> # Dogs Don't Speak English

Wendy Nelson Crann
Executive Director Working Animals Giving Serice For Kids

Illustrated by
JoAnn Lowe

© Copyright 2006 by Wendy Nelson Crann

ISBN 0-9768477-1-X

Library of Congress
2010940622

Second Printing
2010

Book Design by
Ron Humphrey

All rights reserved. No part of this book may be reproduced or transmitted in any form without written permission of the author, except by reviewers who may quote brief excerpts in connection with a review.

Windjammer Adventure Publishing
289 South Franklin Street, Chagrin Falls, OH 44022
Telephone 440.247.6610 Email windjammerpub@mac.com

DEDICATED..........

To families looking for the tools to find a dog, train a dog and make him all they need him to be.

To teach any dog owner what is possible.

To my husband Eddie, whose support makes it possible for me to do the work I love.

To my daughter Sera.

To my dad, Bud.

Our beautiful illustrations are
dedicated by the artist.
To Jenny — a shining example of pure love.

THE INMATE TRAINERS OF NORTH CENTRAL CORRECTIONAL INSTITUTION

Take a group of people with no experience in training animals and arm them with the best dog training information available. Select puppies for them to work with that are excellent in temperament and attention to learn. What could you expect to happen? What we expected and, in fact have developed, is the "Cell Dog" training program for the Working Animals Giving Service for Kids charity.

A select group of inmates were chosen to house and train potential service animals while adhering strictly to the best possible training protocol for the animals. You may have seen our, or similar programs discussed on television. The Accredited Apprenticeship Training Program in conjunction with the Ohio Department of Rehabilitation and Corrections is written here.

This is the program we wrote and use to prepare mobility service and skilled companion animals for children in Northeast Ohio. This is our philosophy of training, our understanding of how dogs learn and our method of kindness and consistency. It was written so that even those with little or no experience could have excellent results. This book starts at the very beginning, with choosing the right puppy, and has been edited over years of use with the input of the actual inmate trainers who work with the dogs every day.

For each of the men of NCCI chosen to participate as primary handlers of a WAGS dog, there are two or more men waiting in the wings. These secondary handlers study, practice and learn our training methods, waiting for a dog to become available and their own chance to train a dog that will change a child's life. It is a drive to do something completely for the good of another and perhaps, a chance to give back for what each has done in his past. This is what keeps these men involved and dedicated to the work they do.

Working Animals Giving Service For Kids, Inc.

W.A.G.S. 4 Kids is a non profit 501(c)(3) charity dedicated to providing certified service and skilled companion animals to children with mobility disabilities and life crisis medical conditions. The ability of a service dog to advance his partner's dignity, independence and quality of life is irrefutable. We meet the needs of real people by providing better access to and increased availability of service and skilled companion animals.

Our special interest is in children. We focus on the needs of children, too young by most organizations' standards to be considered for partnership with a dog. We believe in early intervention and the power of that special bond between a child and a dog. We work with families so that these animals, certified in the parent's name, can be a constant support in their child's life and help them overcome social barriers.

The following training techniques and requirements are those used by W.A.G.S. 4 Kids in the progression of skills training from the time a puppy is selected for service training. W.A.G.S. 4 Kids selects and trains both pure bred and mixed breed animals based on the successful completion of temperament testing. Animals are acquired from purchase and donations by select breeders and from rescue organizations. As an overview, puppies are started on the "naming" of behaviors from their first interactions. House breaking begins at ten weeks. Command training begins at approximately fourteen weeks.

The importance of "naming" cannot be stressed enough. The W.A.G.S. 4 Kids program allows for several weeks of the naming process before any command training is to begin. The basis of a dog's ability to learn specific tasks is by naming a behavior consistently so that recognition develops. There is no short cut that produces equal results.

Some behaviors or body positions must be stimulated by luring the dog with a treat. This will create an opportunity to name the behavior for him. Luring is only used for exercises where it would be unlikely for the animal to initiate the desired behavior on his own.

Because this manual was written with the goals of service work in mind, there are references to commands and/or exercises that may not be of interest to pet only trainers. In particular, the **go to work** command was specifically written with the needs of a service dog. This exercise may be translated by a pet owner to the activity of leashing your dog. You may, however, choose to omit it.

For owners of pets who are no longer puppies, even for pets who are well past puppy status, our message is positive. You can teach old dogs new tricks. You can improve your dog's behavior by changing your own. Your own behavior can change when you understand how your pet is best able to learn from you.

SPECIAL THANKS

To Sargeant Teri Jolliff and the staff of the North Central Correctional Institution, Marion, Ohio

To the inmate trainers of NCCI and their committment to learn, train, teach and excel.

To our artist's models
Abby & Moby
Laurie & Keebler
Bob, Steve, Mike and their Goldens

TABLE OF CONTENTS

Preface xii
Adoption Is Serious Business 1
   Count to Ten 2
Basic Training 11
   Training Skills List 13
      "No's" 13
      Kennel 14
      Furniture 15
      People Food 15
      Naming 16
      Talking 16
      Love and Attention 17
      Look 18
   The First Twenty Weeks 21
      Housebreaking 21
      "OW" Training 26
      Kennel In 28
      On A Leash 28
      Grooming 31
      Place 33
      Heeling 34
      Exercise 36
      Vocalizing 38
      Teething 39
      Toys 40
      Traveling in the Car 41
   Common Behavior Modifications 43
      Nipping 43
      Barking 45

Pawing For Attention 46

Pawing/Digging 47

Solitary Destruction 48

Special Notes 49

Commands 51

The Beginning Commands 53

Come 53

Sit 53

Down 54

Go To Work 54

Look 55

Gaining Control 57

Heeling with Sit 57

Stay 57

Jump up/Jump off 58

Lap 59

Upping the Ante 60

Leave it 60

Wait 60

The Key to Retrieving 63

Take it 63

Hold it 63

Drop it 64

Give it 65

Bring it 65

Body Positions 67

Finish/Stand 67

Variations of Stay 68

Position Practice 69

- **More Body Positions** 70
  - Side 70
  - Back 70
  - Follow 71
- **Going the Distance** 73
  - Distance Commands 73
  - Go Commands 74
- **Things to Know** 75
- **Intermediate Training** 77
  - Working Off Leash 79
  - Stairs 81
  - Bracing 83
  - Tug 86
  - Hit and Touch 88
  - Out In The World 92
  - Distractions 96
  - Weaning From Treats 103
- **Advanced Training Skills** 107
  - Compound Directions 107
  - Tug Command Skills 108
  - Hit and Touch Command Skills 111
  - Retrieval 114
  - Emergency Procedures 120
  - Public Transportation 124
  - How Compound Can Directions Be . . . 127
- **A Final Thought** 131

PREFACE

I once had a friend named Gary, an experienced dog trainer, who decided as a clever demonstration of his own abilities, to train his dog basic obedience commands with the names of colors. Each color meant something to Clark, the Springer Spaniel. The pair showed off feats of sit, stay, down, come and the grand finale of balancing a small dog biscuit on Clark's nose until told to "take it". The commands for these activities were recited in the colors of the rainbow as my friend the trainer called out "red, blue, green, yellow and purple".

The idea for this experiment began from a conversation Gary and I often had about how people spent way too much time blabbing to their pets. Engaging in whole conversations the poor pooch couldn't possibly understand. It just wouldn't matter what words a person chose to command their dog to sit. They could call sitting "jellybeans" if so inspired because as long as the verbal command was attached in the same way to the same behavior all the time, eventually anyone could say "jellybeans" and the dog would sit. Our conversation, repeated in some fashion on and off for years had caught Gary's fancy, I suppose, and it was some time later that I was introduced to Clark and his colorful repertoire.

In the end it was simply a comical waste of time on Gary's part. The fact is, a well trained animal should respond to anyone in a position of control equally as well as he behaves for the trainer. Skills attached to a command word should transfer to anyone using the same word with the dog. Using Gary's system, no one else could control old Clark. We couldn't remember if "red" was down or stay, if "blue" was come or wait to take the cookie on your nose.

We did wind up learning the importance of training your dog with words or hand signals that anyone would commonly associate with the skill you want your dog to perform. That, however, is for the benefit of the people your pet will come in contact with. As Gary and I decided years ago, it doesn't matter to your dog, because dogs don't speak English.

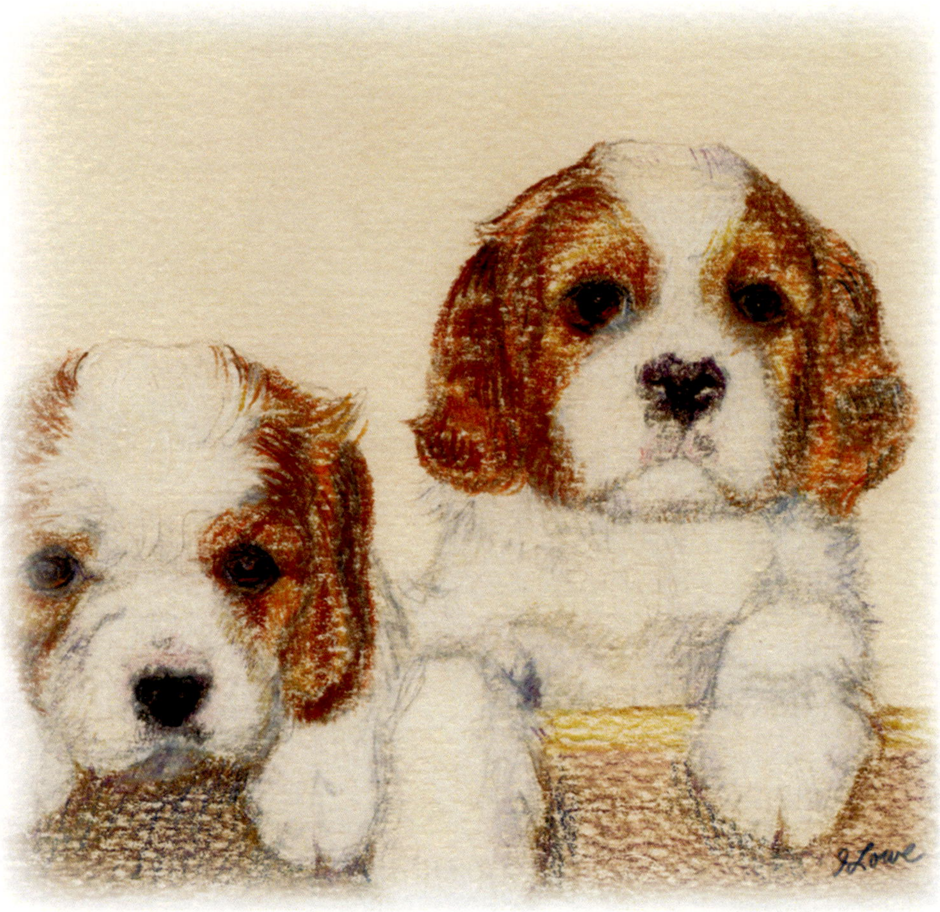

ADOPTION IS SERIOUS BUSINESS

If you are a single person, choosing your dog can be like picking out your new best friend. This is going to be the one you come home to every night, share your free time with, and in some ways, to whom you give up your freedom. No more darting out to meet your friends after work. You'll have to go home and take the dog out first!

Adopting a dog into a family can set an example for good behavior for a child's lifetime. How you treat this pet will be a child's tangible experience in love, patience, responsibility, handling adversity and the list goes on.

I think everyone should have a dog. I actually think everyone should have two. I think every child should grow up learning the lessons animal ownership can teach. Unfortunately, I am wrong. Not everyone or every family has the temperament or time needed to succeed in that relationship. There is a lot to consider first. My best advice is to be sure and think through the consequences of bringing a living and sometimes demanding addition into your household. Read all of this book before decisions are made. Decide what you want and what is possible. Before you rush out and do something in haste, take a deep breath and count to ten.

COUNT TO TEN

ONE

Don't buy a puppy today. Wait a week. You have a lot of work to do first.

Successful ownership and training is rooted in all the decisions you should be making before your dog joins the family. Forget about how cute the furry little bundle looks. The puppy won't look like that for long and in about 10 months, for every day of the next eight to eighteen years, that adorable little pup is going to look like a full grown whatever it is you've decided on. Your first decision is what kind of adult dog you want to live with.

TWO

Go to the library, not the pet store.

The American Kennel Club has done a lot of the homework for you. They have compiled a guide full of the most important information about each recognized pure breed. Look at their guide and others you find at the library. Pay particular attention to pictures of adult dogs in each breed. Read about the traits and the descriptions of the dogs that appeal to you. All of this information will help you make the decisions that are to follow.

THREE

How much room do you have and how much of it are you willing to give up?

Big feet need big shoes and big dogs need big everything: big walks, big backyards, big beds, big bowls and big bags of dog food. I love big dogs. But even if your current living space is big, do you want to share it with a whole lot of dog? If you are likely to move, will owning a large dog limit or eliminate options of where you may be able to live in the future? There are many small and medium sized breeds that may make a better choice for you.

FOUR
Let's talk about hard wiring.

Temperament is the term we use to discuss the demeanor and behavior of a dog. It's like the hard wiring of the dog's brain. How would the dog react normally, left to his own choosing? Temperament is important because that's what you start with on the road to training your dog. Whatever you want your dog to do or be is fine. Picking one whose temperament is a match with your expectations will make life easier.

Even with a pure bred dog, no one can guarantee a disposition just like the one described by any book. A breed guide will outline tendencies of a particular breed and that's a good place to start. When choosing to have a mixed breed in your home, understand that you can't expect to get a 50/50 split on the temperament traits of each side of the puppy's background. It's a genetic tumble that could turn out any way at all. There are lots of great mixed breed dogs. You're just starting out with less specific information when you begin training.

FIVE
Trimming, brushing, shedding...enough said.

My heart belongs to a Golden Retriever who sheds enough hair to stuff furniture. All dogs need grooming. All dogs shed. You need to decide how much you are willing to do, how much you are willing to pay someone else to do, or how little grooming the breed of dog you choose will need.

SIX
Do you really want a puppy?

By now you've made the decisions that will help you choose what breed or mixed breed dog will fit best into your household and lifestyle. Ask yourself now, do you really want a puppy? I know you want a dog, but do you want to start your ownership experience with a puppy? The big differences, of course, are housebreaking and teething. These are necessary, unavoidable, time consuming tasks that might be already accomplished by adopting a somewhat older dog.

SEVEN
It's time for a family meeting.

If you live alone that will cut down on the arguments. The fact is, everyone in the household needs to agree in advance of the dog's arrival exactly what it is you expect.

Where will the dog sleep?

Where will the dog go to the bathroom?

What parts of your home will be accessible to the dog?

Where, when and how will the dog be confined?

Will you allow the dog to "kiss" you on the face?

Will anyone be allowed to feed the dog "people" food?

Will the dog be allowed on the furniture?

Ask questions of each other about what you expect and answer them before you bring a pet home. If you have children too young to participate in adhering to the decisions of the family, choosing an older dog whose basic skills are already intact may be an option.

EIGHT
Divide the labor.

Work shared will make each person's burden lighter. It also fosters a feeling of equal importance to and ownership of the animal. If Mom is the only one who feeds the pup you're likely to wind up with a one person dog. Walking, feeding, grooming, backyard clean up and more.

It all has to be done and certainly some jobs are less desirable than others. You might use a chart for chore duty that rewards a week of poop scooping with a week of sleeping with the puppy. Move chores around as equally as possible. Decide before you bring the dog home who will be doing what and then stick to it.

NINE

The big question is, are you ready for the long haul?

The bounce back rate on puppies is appalling. Can you imagine a Great Dane breed rescue group reporting that the most common reason 6 to 12 month old Danes are relinquished by their owners is that they just didn't realize how big the dog would get? Boy, they didn't do their homework! Some Toy breeds live to be 18 years old or older. Are you ready for that long a commitment?

TEN

You've waited a week. You've done your homework. Let's go get a dog!

Keep in mind the two most important factors in choosing your puppy. The first is *conformation*, or how the dog is built. We're looking for a dog that is soundly built with all parts working. The second factor is *temperament*. This is how the dog behaves with you, toward the other dogs in the litter and when left alone.

The best predictor of a puppy's conformation is in the genetic line of his parents. That is why, without a doubt, the best place to buy a pure bred dog is from an AKC registered show quality breeder. This is someone who is actively participating in showing his own dogs, because that will mean he is breeding dogs carefully to produce the soundest, best quality dogs possible for his own use. He will usually pick one or two of the puppies to keep and watch for show potential and sell the rest of the litter. How lucky for you. You have the opportunity to have a pure bred dog with the same fine genetic breeding. For show purposes, their flaw may be as minor as a patch of white fur on a breed that requires one uniform color.

Breeders with "pet only" litters of pups may be using AKC registered dogs, but are not breeding for show quality and are not necessarily as concerned about flaws, though minor, that may continue to pass along through their generations of breeding. Try to avoid buying from breeders who over use a female with multiple litters of puppies in the same year or are breeding year after year with the same pair of dogs.

Don't be fooled by breeders selling "designer" breeds. Cockapoos and Labradoodles aren't pure bred dogs. There is nothing wrong with wanting one, simply understand that they are mixed breeds. The breeder may know specifically what two disparate breeds were used to produce the puppy. It's still a genetic mystery as to which traits of each breed the puppy will inherit. If you are looking for a mixed breed dog, you might think about saving a life in the process and visit your local Animal Protective League.

Pet stores don't breed dogs. They buy dogs from breeders, mark the price up and sell them to you. I know of no show quality breeder who sells his puppies through a pet store, not one.

Owning a mixed breed puppy is a choice many people make. A very good reason to make that choice is to save a life. A not so good reason is because the puppy looks cute (remember, puppies only look like puppies for a few months), or you've decided that today is the day you're going to get a dog (remember, you're supposed to do your homework and wait a week). Local animal shelters and rescue groups rely on the good will of adoptive families. I have owned and trained some wonderful mixed breeds.

The most important part in selecting a mixed breed puppy is understanding that because there is no reliable genetic information, you must look toward your own ability to size up the pup. What you can have working for you are a variety of temperament tests to determine the behavior tendencies of any puppy you are interested in, whether mixed or pure bred.

Watch the puppy as it interacts with other puppies. Is it a bully? Does the puppy sit listlessly in a corner while the others play? What you would like to see is behavior that demonstrates an active interest in group play. Is the pup aggressive over food or toys? Is he growling? Do not accept this behavior as something a puppy will "grow out of".

Ask that any one dog you are interested in be separated from the group. Have a toy in the solitary area for the puppy to play with. Watch the puppy as it is alone. Does he whine, pace, jump, or show signs of anxiety? Is he able to settle himself and find interest in a toy?

Sit on the floor with the puppy and tap the floor in front of you gently. Does the puppy come to you playfully or aggressively and biting? Does he ignore your presence? Is he fearful of you? Lower yourself onto the floor and while lying there, encourage the puppy's attention toward you with tapping or clapping noises. Does the puppy pounce on your head and back to play, or does he squirm under you to be playful from a more passive position?

Is the puppy interested in your attention above other distractions? Roll a ball across the floor for the puppy to follow. As he moves toward the ball with normal puppy curiosity, tap your fingers on the floor, clap your hands lightly or make a kissing noise. Just make some noise that would attract the puppy's attention back toward you. You are looking to see the puppy give up his interest in the rolling object and turn back to you. A puppy that has no interest in following the object at all, one that won't leave your side to investigate a thrown toy, may not be a good choice. He may be too clingy, have fear issues or simply not be interested in the world around him.

Another good test is to see if the puppy has fear of startling noises. I'm sure you know someone with a dog too afraid of the vacuum cleaner to stay in the room on cleaning day. Test the puppy by dropping a metal object on the floor. If you're really thorough, you could bring a small dust buster to plug in. It's perfectly natural for a puppy to turn and show interest in the noise. We would even like to see the puppy move toward the object to quietly investigate. It would be less desirable for the dog to squeal, run in fear, urinate, bark or vocalize in any way.

Pick the puppy up in your arms. A little happy puppy squirming is a good thing, but flailing and trying to escape from you is not. Grasp the puppy's body under his front legs and lift him so that his feet are slightly off the floor. His body should be still, not unable to come to rest. The stillness should be evident through the entire length of the body. A twitching tail shows nervousness even if the upper body is resigned. Try to make eye contact with him. Will he not look you in the eye? We want good eye contact. This will indicate his ability, or the lack of it, to pay attention to you and all the training that is to follow. Turn the puppy on his back slowly and cradle him like a baby. He should be able to lie quietly in your arms and hopefully will be able to look at you if you encourage him with a little clicking or kissing noise.

Lastly, place the puppy on the ground lying on his side. Apply some pressure to the pup's body at the shoulder and hip, pressing firmly enough for the puppy to feel confined, but not so strongly as to inflict discomfort. Again, we are looking for willing acceptance from the dog. Take your time with all of these movements and body position changes. Move slowly to get the best, most accurate responses in the puppy's behavior. When puppies, like people, show you who they are, believe them. Spare yourself years of problem behavior by allowing the puppy to show his true temperament and personality to you. Both you and the pup deserve a great relationship right from the start. If the shoe doesn't fit, wait until you find one that does.

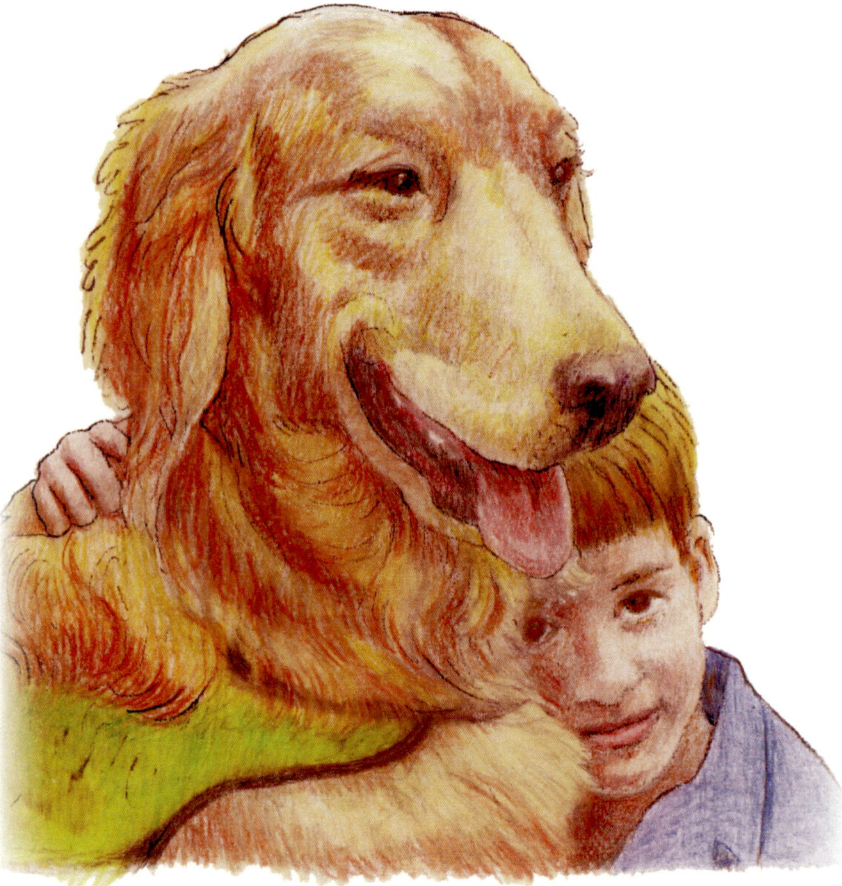

BASIC TRAINING

The one most important skill you must acquire as a trainer is to understand how any dog will be able to learn what it is you want the dog to know. *Dogs don't speak English.* Repeat that fact to yourself often. Standing in front of your newly adopted dog saying the words "sit, sit, sit" might as well be the noise from a vacuum cleaner to a dog's ears. Dogs learn from body language, from behavior and the behavior's consequences. Conversations are meant for your kids, your best friend, your spouse — not the dog.

Understand that you own and control all of the things your dog wants in life. The big two are food and your attention. These are the tools we use as rewards for training and repeating approved behaviors. The other side of the reward coin is not punishment. We want the dog to self correct his behaviors, not to be afraid of your wrath. Self correction is always the highest level of a dog's training. The opposite response on your part to giving a reward is called deprivation. You will withhold your attention and you will monitor training treats to define and reinforce the behaviors you want your dog to repeat. Be clear that training treats are tiny morsels not whole dog biscuits. We use a small piece of dry dog food, some brand other than our regular mealtime fare, as the treat. In this way we can maintain a healthy diet and simply subtract the treat food volume from the dog's daily mealtime food allotment.

No rawhides or edible toys of any kind are allowed. Treats are given to mark and reinforce a behavior that we want the dog to learn, something we want the dog to be able to do each time we use a specific command word or hand sign. Wait to give a treat until the dog is doing exactly what you want. There are no treats for behavior that is "almost." Be specific in what you reward and then you are clearly teaching the animal what it is you want.

You are the dog's leader and mentor for all of the

wonderful and useful things he will know. Never engage in tug of war games or any game you might one day lose. No chasing games unless he is chasing you. You go through doors first and you make the decisions. You will teach him where, when, how and who.

Training Skills List

YOU CAN'T TEACH "NO'S"

As a private obedience instructor, the one most common circumstance I faced upon meeting a new client was to be given a list of things the dog owner did not want his pet to do. There was to be no jumping, no begging for food at the table, no getting on the sofa in the living room and the list went on. The fact is, you can't teach a dog what not to do. It is a big joke in our family that a once beloved pet, Sadie, always jolted up from her nap on our sofa and jumped off the minute anyone came into the room. My mother always remarked, "See, Sadie knows she's not allowed on the furniture". Truth be told, Sadie really only knew to get off the sofa when someone came by. She never learned not to get up there in the first place. We need to have our dogs "self correct," to learn the rules and monitor their behavior whether we are in the room or not. Any instance of self correction is the highest level training moment your dog can have. Always strive for a training exercise of self correction.

We need our dogs to learn not to get on the furniture instead of getting off when the threat of discipline is near. The only way to teach a dog not to do behaviors you *don't* approve of is by training and reinforcing the things you *do* want him to do. If your dog is trained to stay out of the kitchen or to be lying on a mat or dog bed when you are sitting at the table for meals, then there is no question that he will not be begging for food at the table.

For each of the things you have decided you will not allow your animal to do, you must translate the training exercise into what you do want your dog to be doing instead. The plan you make for exactly what you want your dog to be doing is your intention for all the training that is to follow. Whatever that plan is, remember that dogs learn best in small doses. A two minute session ten times a day is a far better training approach than one twenty minute marathon. Puppies need to build up their attention spans and learn the language you are teaching them. Overworking your pup can make him lose focus and feel that he will never please you. The result may cause frustration for you and a pup unwilling and uninterested in working. Avoid this by making sure to begin and end all training sessions at a moment of success, however small.

KENNEL

A crate or kennel is a required training tool for housebreaking. In addition, when used properly, it is a secure and safe place for rest and confinement for the lifetime of the dog. Think of the kennel as your dog's private bedroom, a space he will grow to love and seek out. Our adult dogs continue to go to their kennels for rest even though they have earned run of the house privileges. The kennel doors are open and the dogs choose to nap there. Training to a kennel must never be a punishment. It is his sanctuary.

The kennel should be placed in a temperate, low distraction area of the home. Don't put the kennel in the middle of the kitchen and expect to achieve training success while scurrying around trying to fix dinner. Your best bet in purchasing a crate is to take advantage of the adjustable dividers that come with many wire crate models. That way, you can invest in the purchase of one crate to accommodate the adult size of the dog you have chosen and by using the divider accessory, separate off just the portion your growing puppy needs as the months progress. A puppy in training needs only enough room to stand, turn around and settle himself back down. A crate that is too large will defeat the purpose of the housebreaking task that is to follow.

When it is time for your puppy to be confined, make sure you consistently name the action of the dog entering the crate. We use "kennel in", but any language is all right. A treat may be used to lure the pup into the kennel. If a lure is not needed and the pup enters willingly then be sure to offer the treat after the kennel is closed. The whole experience must be calm and positive. Lay or sit next to the kennel so that the pup can feel your presence. You may even put a finger or two inside the kennel. Don't speak, simply remain there until the puppy has settled down for a nap. The next time remain a little farther away from the kennel as the puppy settles down for a nap and proceed with kennel training by gradually moving farther away from the kennel each time.

Resist the temptation to have the puppy fall into napping outside of the kennel. When it's time for a rest, the kennel is where you should put him. It is after training to a confined place to sleep has been successful that you may invite other behaviors. Remember, babies must learn to sleep in their own beds first. It is cruel to allow a tiny pup to consistently fall asleep on your belly or in your bed and then, when you've changed your mind, to have him wind up sleeping alone in the basement.

NO FURNITURE

It is unreasonable to expect a dog to know the difference between approved and disapproved furniture. We must train for the possibility that a dog's life partner may have some physical reason to preclude jumping on beds or chairs. Much later, after the dog is well trained and obedient you may invite the animal to join you on the furniture, if you must. A better habit is to come down to the dog's level on the floor for cuddles. This, I am afraid, includes refraining from holding dogs on your lap while you are sitting on furniture.

NO PEOPLE FOOD

NEVER....Unless otherwise directed by a veterinarian, there is simply no reason to include "people" food in the dog's diet. Furthermore, it is unreasonable to expect a dog to learn the skills and adapt to the necessary behaviors for inclusion out in the world of temptation once he is placed with a partner. He must learn right from the start that people food is never for him. Training begins at the family's mealtime with the dog in a down position while people are eating. To insure success, leash your dog and place your foot on the leash very near the collar. Here is your first perfect example of a self corrective training moment. You foot is on the leash so if the dog tries to get up he will, by necessity, have to resettle himself down. From your part, no discussion, no attention, no correction. The dog will self correct his behavior. Name the position "down" as the dog lies on the floor under the dining table. Treats should never be given during mealtime training. Wait until the exercise is completed and then call the dog away from the table. If the puppy is very young, he should be napping in his kennel during family meal times.

NAMING

Training is simply identifying approved behaviors, naming them as they occur with a word and/or sign and repeating the process until recognition occurs. Naming is the prerequisite to all command training. You must be aware and ever watchful of the dog's behaviors. Each time your puppy sits down, name the behavior for him, ***sit***. As he walks toward you for meal time, for attention, name this for him, ***come***. Tell him when he lays down, ***down***. Name everything, all the time, in the exact word that matches the behavior. We call it our *Rule of Ten Thousand Times*. After Ten Thousand Times we'll start to ask and expect our dog to recognize the name we have given to his behaviors and to perform them on command. This applies to all of your training intentions. We name in exactly the same way for each of the things you expect your dog to do.

DON'T TALK TOO MUCH

Remember that your animal doesn't speak English. Every word needs to be attached to a behavior: No baby talk, no blah, blah, blah, no babble. Your voice must carry importance. Don't use language to correct unacceptable behavior. We do not train with the word "no". Use instead a distractive noise to stop the behavior and regain control by giving the dog some approved behavior to do. A distractive noise can be shaking coins in a tin can, dropping a pan on the floor, anything to startle and redirect the dog's attention. We use a gruff and explosive sounding vocal, "eh, eh, eh" as a distraction—we just never seem to have a can of coins around when we need one. When you do address your dog, be aware of the tone of voice you choose. High pitched voices encourage enthusiastic, energetic behavior. That would be a good choice for an exercise such as **come**. Low tones generate a more calm demeanor. Think of this in exercises for **down** and **stay**.

GIVE NO LOVE OR ATTENTION UNLESS THE DOG IS SITTING OR LYING DOWN

With no words at all you can train your dog quiet restraint and patience. You can instill the kind of self

Sitting for attention

control that precludes any tendency toward jumping or demanding behavior. From your first interactions with

a dog you are teaching the animal what is acceptable behavior. Raise your expectations. Should your dog approach you and begin to jump, simply turn away from him. Do not engage him in the "No, down, off" game. By responding verbally to bad jumping behavior, you have in effect allowed the animal to get what he wants, which is your attention. By turning away and giving the animal no attention at all, you are reinforcing the requirement of his self correcting to calm patience in order to gain your attention. Continue to turn away, again and again, until the dog has tired and settled himself. The key is to lavish praise and attention when the dog sits down and performs as you wish.

LOOK

Every word we say to our animal must be the name of a behavior. That rule includes the dog's name. The behavior

Look

we are announcing with the name of the dog is to gain his attention, to say *look at me*. With the dog sitting in front of you, **say the dog's name** while moving your index finger from his nose toward your nose. That is speciffically the meaning of your dog's name. "Fido" means **look at me.** In order to teach your dog anything you must have his attention. As your gaze connects, say **look** and reward with a treat. The dog's eyes will naturally follow the movement of your finger. You may even begin practicing this exercise with the treat in the same hand you are using to point between his nose and yours. This first step, training your dog to give you his full attention, we call being "on task". We at all times, require the dog to be giving attention to his trainer not the reward or treat in the trainer's hand. Once you have command of your dog's attention with his own name, you are on the road to control of all the other command training to follow.

Dogs Don't Speak English

The First Twenty Weeks

HOUSEBREAKING

Entire books have been written on the subject of housebreaking. The fact is, you will never truly love or appreciate an animal that is soiling your home. Except for the instance of illness, there are no such things as "accidents" to a trained animal. A dog is either housebroken or he is not. Your first tool in housebreaking is a feeding schedule. Free feeding does not help to promote good and reliable potty habits. Clinically speaking, it's very hard to plan on when lunch is coming out one end if you don't know when it went in the other. The same applies to liquids. Young puppies, eating three or four meals a day, can be expected to have a bowel movement for each time they eat, plus one. Next, there is little point in trying to housebreak a puppy too young. If you wait to pick up your puppy until he is 8 or preferably 10 weeks old you'll have a much more successful experience. The final element is you. You must bring a puppy into your home when you have the time to housebreak. There is no substitute for consistency. The lack of it will be *your* fault, not the dog's.

Go Potty

Before the dog comes home decide the following: Where will the kennel be? What door will you be consistently using as the dog's exit to the outside bathroom area? What word name will you be consistently using to signify the activity? You may choose to train with two words; one for urination and another to encourage a bowel movement. Next, be prepared to reward the approved behavior outside while it's happening. That means take the treats outside with you and use them at the point of success. Dogs trained with a reward the moment upon returning into the house will get the idea that coming inside is the approved behavior. These are dogs that may continually "ask" to go outside. It's not really because they have an urgency to relieve themselves, more likely it's to be given a treat when they come back inside.

Bring your puppy home early in the day, not in the evening. This simply will give you an entire day to immediately begin presenting the day's schedule to the pup. The schedule is what will regulate his bathroom needs. A good starting schedule is feeding three meals: 7AM, noon and 5PM. We wean down to two meals at approximately 12 weeks by gradually adding more food to the morning and evening meal as we diminish the volume from the noon meal. Our animals remain on two meals a day for their lifetime.

The schedule is simple. Confinement begins in the kennel for a nap. When the puppy wakes, or better yet, when you wake the puppy up, immediately pick him up, attach his leash and carry him directly outside through the one and only door you will be using for his bathroom experience. Put him on the ground where you want him to go, and use your naming word. Give the dog his treat and praise right there, just as he completes urinating.

A young pup will usually have a bowel movement ten to thirty minutes after mealtime. Engage in quiet interactions after the meal and when ready, repeat the bathroom process, carrying him while attached on a leash, through the same door, naming the activity and treating when successful. For a bowel movement, the pup may want to sniff around a bit. Make sure you have carried the puppy to the area you will want him to use outside. Once you have put him on the ground he will be able to wander a bit on the leash. Make sure you don't move with him. Be like a tree and stand your ground. If this is the area you want the dog to use, then this is where you stay. The puppy will have plenty of roaming room in a circle around you on the end of a standard, six foot leash.

Keep up the process without deviation. The puppy's day will likely be: wake up; out to urinate; breakfast; quiet interaction; bowel movement; rough and tumble play; nap in kennel; up and out to urinate; lunch; quiet interaction; bowel movement, and so on. While this may not be exact, it will be close. Some puppies wake up in the morning having a bowel movement on their first trip outside. This will probably mean that after breakfast another movement will be somewhat later in the mid morning. Some pups have a last, pre-bed movement even though dinner and a movement were right on schedule at 5PM. Be aware that these individual tendencies will present themselves.

Help your pup stay dry all night in the kennel by not offering more liquids four hours before his last out of the evening. Make sure the kennel is sized to allow the dog just enough room to turn around and resettle himself during sleep. Dogs have a natural desire to keep their sleep area unsoiled. A kennel too large will only encourage a dog to soil one area of the kennel and escape to the other end to sleep. During this process it is wise to refrain from bundling your puppy's kennel with blankets or pillows for cuddling. You'll only be providing him with an opportunity to begin passive chewing habits and providing yourself with lots of laundry to wash as the puppy has an accident or two.

If the kennel is soiled, you must clean and disinfect it thoroughly and bathe the pup as well. Dogs allowed to live in and be confined to dirty places grow accustomed to this.

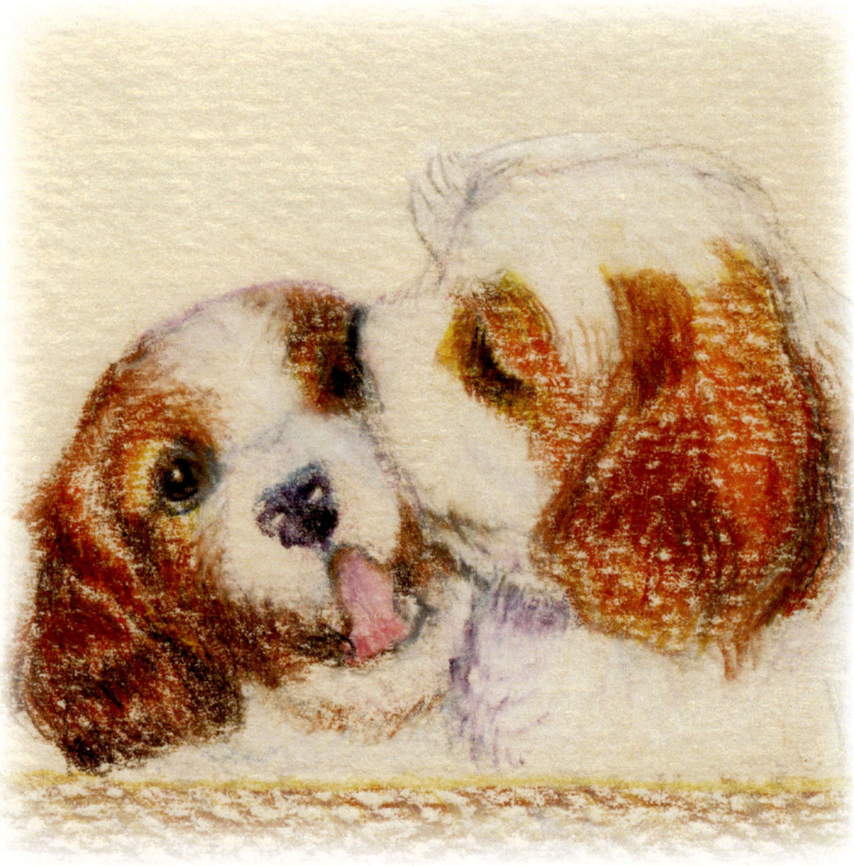

You will be altering your pup's natural aversion to keep his area clean if you do not sanitize completely. It is far better to limit the bottom of the crate to a neatly folded newspaper, with no edges exposed for chewing, or even nothing in the crate at all. Remember, we are training the dog to **hold it**. Keep your expectations appropriate to the age of the dog. By the time a pup is 12 weeks old, he should be dry through the night and for periods of three to four hours during the day if his liquid intake is properly regulated.

Never remove the dog from the crate if he is whining or barking in demand. Wait for a moment of quiet and then name ***quiet*** as you remove him to go outside. Lastly, there is a learning curve to be expected. That's the part that is up to you. Be watchful of sniffing or squatting behaviors in the house so that you may be at the ready to scoop the dog up with a distractive noise, take him immediately outside to the appropriate area, name and reward the bathroom behavior with a treat. These instances of accident that you catch before they happen are the very best training moments the dog can have. These are the moments that are direct consequences of the dog's behavior. Consequences of behavior are the most effective training tools we have.

A dry crate overnight means the dog is crate trained, not "house broken". Initiate freedom in limited areas, beginning with one room at a time. Start with a room the family spends lots of time in. You'll be teaching your dog that this space is his home and not to be soiled, much in the same way he doesn't soil the crate he sleeps in.

Add additional rooms one at a time, practicing his going out routine from this new space, out through his designated door. The ultimate test is to announce **Let's go potty** from any room in your home and have the dog head, on his own, to the correct door—that's a house broken dog and one that is ready for the privilege of freedom. If you choose to continue the practice of a designated bathroom area outside, you may name that area as well. We use ***potty spot***, as in **Let's go potty spot**. The dogs ultimately go to that same area each time.

"OW" TRAINING

This is, more accurately, a series of exercises that will condition your animal to readily accept the bumps and bruises of life without ever reacting badly. We call it "kid proofing" the dog. These exercises will be performed over an extended period of time to produce a safe and reliable reaction from the dog under any circumstance.

Opening a dog's mouth

Begin by keeping your hand or finger in the dog's dish at meal times. If you have chosen the puppy well, in that he had shown no signs of food aggression, he will accept your hand in his food. At any sign of objection to your presence there, simply pick up the dish and start again until he is able to calmly eat around your fingers. Next, practice removing food from the pup's mouth while he is eating. Start with giving him a small treat and then fishing it out of his mouth before he has the chance to chew it. Name this, ***open*** as you open his mouth to take it. Always do this particular exercise a few times in a row so that the puppy gets used to this mouth invasion. End the exercise by allowing the pup to have the treat.

Training a passive response to food is the number one way to keep children safe around your animal. Repeat this training as it pertains to approved dog toys. The dog may have the toy when and as you say. Do not engage in any tug of war with toys, not ever. Tug games promote aggressive behaviors. As your puppy grows larger, tug is a game he may one day win. Simply name **open** as you open the dog's mouth and remove the toy, again ending the exercise with allowing the dog to keep the toy.

Our last series of exercises pertain to body responses: tugging of ears, feet, tails, putting fingers in the dog's ears and nostrils—all the accidents of life that may happen when you pair kids with dogs. These introductions to unpleasant body contacts begin very gently. First, make sure the pup will tolerate being touched everywhere, particularly inside and out of his mouth and ears. Hold, stroke and press his feet, lift his tail. All of this should be done daily, while holding a small treat for the pup to keep his attention. Practice holding the pup still in your arms and on his side and belly on the ground with slight pressure. Release him with a treat. Only after several weeks of success do we begin adding a small tug or unexpected insertion of fingers at the end of the exercise. Remember to release the treat to your dog at the point of slight discomfort. Our goal, of course, is to have a dog readily accept some discomfort in life with no more reaction than, "where's my treat?"

KENNEL IN

You have been naming the kennel each time the dog has been made to enter, leading with a treat. The next step is to toss the treat into the crate and name **kennel in** as the puppy follows. Now we will begin to send the dog into the kennel with a hand sign. Extend your index finger and swing your arm in the direction of the opened kennel door. It will look to the pup as if you are tossing the treat inside as before. Name **kennel in** and give the treat after the dog has entered. Continue practicing this hand sign from further distances away from the kennel door and reward with a treat once the dog has entered.

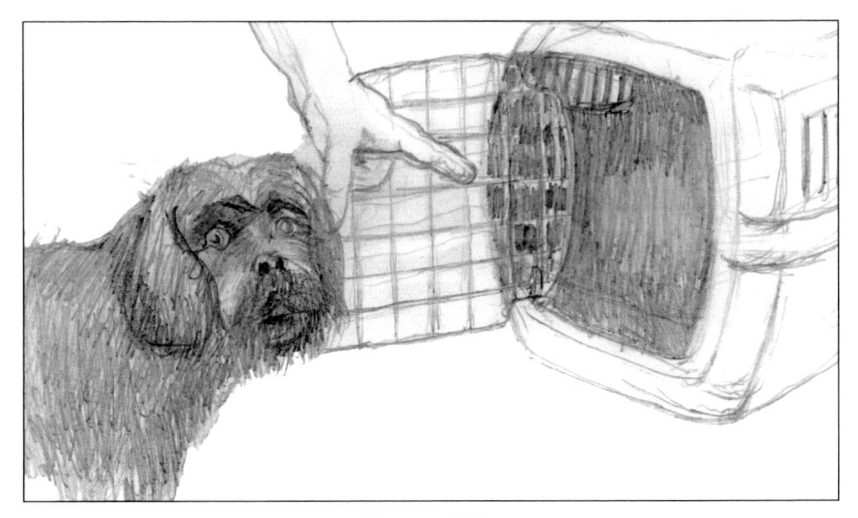

Kennel In

ON A LEASH

The prerequisite to heel training is to get the puppy used to being on leash, and used to being in the approved position relative to your body. The heel position is with the dog on your left side, his shoulder on a plane with your hip. Without showing this to the dog he would have no way of knowing this is what you want. Begin to initiate this exercise inside the house before you practice outside. First, let the puppy get used to walking next to you. When you are up and moving around encourage the puppy to walk next to your left side by slapping your left thigh with your hand as you move and perhaps making encouraging clicking or kissing noises. Remember to use a high pitched, enthusiastic tone to hold the puppy's attention and keep moving. As you encourage your pup along, be watchful as he walks. Whenever his body position aligns his shoulder with your left hip name this *heel* and give him a tiny treat.

Monk Leash

The next step is to add a leash attached to his collar to this exercise. You don't have to hold the leash. Rather, let it drag on the floor as the puppy scampers to walk with you. Be sure to name and treat *heel* for the pup when he is in the correct position. Next, take a six foot leash around your waist, tucking the hook end through the loop of the leash handle. Then attach the hook of the leash to the dog's collar. This attachment is called the "monk leash" technique. The end of the dog leash hangs down from your waist resembling the sash of a monk's robe. The collar you choose should fasten comfortably around his neck with a finger or two inserted. Do not use a choke collar on a puppy. With the puppy attached to you, move normally around the house. Your hands will be free to wash the dishes, answer the phone and do other normal household activities. As you move, name and treat the heel position when it occurs naturally. Each time the puppy happens to move with you, his shoulder at your hip, name *heel* and give him a treat. If the puppy has trouble keeping up with you, walk at an adjusted pace for the size of the dog, but keep on moving. It's the dog's job to stay with you. If the puppy walks ahead of you and pulls, stop moving. Come to a complete stop and then change your direction so that you are once again in the lead position. Continue to reinforce this exercise off leash inside the house by tapping your left thigh to encourage the dog to move with you. Name and treat the heel position when it occurs.

GROOMING

Introduced early on, your dog will learn to enjoy daily tooth brushing. Only use toothpaste specifically designed for a dog and never human variety toothpaste. Your dog is not able to spit out the human toothpaste residue and

Grooming

it would certainly give him an upset stomach. Doggie toothpaste is designed to be swallowed and is flavored to encourage your dog to enjoy the experience. Start getting your dog used to brushing by first allowing him to lick a small amount of the paste from your finger. Next, with his understanding of the word ***open***, put a small amount of the paste on your finger, name ***open*** as you put your finger in his mouth and smear the paste on his tooth surface at the gum line. In a few days you will be able to graduate this exercise to the whole mouth, both inside and outside surfaces of the teeth. In the next few weeks, graduate to include a little scrubbing with a rubber finger brush, found at any pet store.

Every day or two the dog's coat should be brushed. The proper brush for your dog is determined by the length of his coat; short coats need a short bristled brush, long coats need a long bristled brush. You may even find a mitt for your hand, with bristles on one side, at your pet store. Your dog will get used to being brushed as easily as he enjoys being stroked by you.

A dog's nails must be clipped both for your comfort as an owner as well as for the health of the dog's feet. Overly long nails encourage bad walking posture for the dog and ultimately can cause a healthy compact paw to splay or widen apart the toes. Learning to cut your dog's nails is not difficult, but should be demonstrated to you by a veterinarian or reputable dog groomer. Once learned, cutting your dog's nails every week or two will allow you to safely make just minor touch ups regularly, rather than long tedious nail cutting sessions. Frequently, once a little weekly trim is part of your dog's routine, he will be very happy to offer each paw for a treat at the end.

PLACE

At your choice, use a mat, towel, blanket, or the like, to signify a spot for the dog to lay and be still when out of

Place

his kennel. Sit there with him, tap the mat and name the area as ***place***, give him treats and attention and affection there. Tell him ***let's go place*** and go there and sit. While engaged there, intermittently tap the mat and say ***place***. Move the mat to different rooms or different spots in the same room and repeat the process, always naming the area ***place***. If you have, up until now, felt you have been depriving your dog of soft bedding in his kennel, the ***place*** exercise will be an opportunity to train his ability to leave alone whatever he is lying on. A blanket or mat in the crate has no chance for survival if the dog can't learn to lie still and not chew on his ***place***.

HEELING

Once the monk leash technique has been successful in moving with your dog inside the home, begin to practice outside. The outside presents many more interesting distractions to the dog and challenges to his attention to you. Keep outside heel training positive and close to home. Practice up and down the driveway. You don't want to get far away from home and have the puppy tire or lose focus and wind up with bad walking behaviors all the way home. Never use a retractable leash. The art of heeling is to keep the dog at your side, not wandering off at a distance. Owners who rely on retractable leashes have, for the most part, never taught their dog to heel. The extended leash just makes it look like the owner wants his animal to be off somewhere instead of walking closely at his side. Practice monk leash techniques outside until your dog clearly understands where his body needs to be when walking. Once this is accomplished you should take the leash from around your waist and begin holding the leash in your hand. Make sure the leash is loose and no tension on your dog's collar exists. Starting with your dog on your left side, swing your left hand and foot out as you announce *heel* with the dog's forward movement. If the dog pulls on the leash give a quick jerk of the leash to gain his attention and remind him to *heel*. If one correction

Heel

does not resolve the pulling, you must come to a complete stop in your forward movement and change direction to reestablish your leadership, as you did with the monk leash. Do not turn heel practice into a contest of strength. As your dog gets older and larger there is a good chance he will win. If heel corrections are anything more than minor adjustments it is a clear sign that you moved too soon to the hand held leash. Inside your home, continue to practice the monk leash technique as well as tapping your thigh and moving with the dog off leash with praise and reward. Outside, monk leash until it is clear that your dog understands the heel position and there will be a very smooth transition.

EXERCISE

Walking your dog isn't the answer. Until your dog has mastered a well positioned heel when walking, other forms of exercise need to be planned. Once a service animal is working with his partner full time, he will very likely spend a great deal of time sitting, waiting for and attending to his partner's needs. The dog's overall health is best maintained with planned, heart pumping, muscle building exercise. Twenty to thirty minutes a day is an excellent habit to maintain. Young puppies can begin with a few five minute sessions and build their endurance to longer exercise periods as they grow.

Walking isn't the answer for two reasons. First, unless you are a very conditioned walker yourself, your pace of walking is probably not brisk enough or done for a long enough duration to really give the dog a good cardio work out. He's only getting to walk as fast as you do. Second, until and unless your animal has mastered the correct **heel** position for walking, walking him on a leash and allowing wandering attention from him or tugging and pulling on the leash is simply an exercise in practicing bad habits. Do **not** use a retractable leash to give him more room to wander. Always promote that his position is by your side.

So, if you can't walk your dog for his planned vigorous exercise, what are you to do? For young puppies, a very good exercise is running toward you. Jog some distance away from your pup and then gain his attention with some enthusiastic hand clapping. As he comes running toward you, you are giving him a great chance to run and giving yourself an opportunity to name **come** for him as he approaches. Give your puppy a chance to exercise by encouraging him to stay with you as you move through your house. Tap your thigh and move briskly, keeping him interested in working to stay at your side as he runs to keep up with you. Remember to name **heel** for him each time his shoulder is positioned correctly on your left side.

As your puppy grows and needs more conditioning, my favorite exercise is simply throwing a ball in the back yard. You get to stay in one place and your dog gets to do the running. You might begin using this opportunity to name his retrieval skills, with **take it** and **give it**. If he is too young, use two or three or more balls for him to chase. Just keep on throwing balls and he will naturally drop the one he has in his mouth to chase after the next one that you throw. Name **drop it** each time he releases a ball from his mouth.

VOCALIZING

One stand out feature of a well trained service animal is his ability to remain calm and quiet regardless of the distraction. We would never select a puppy for training who displays whining or barking behaviors or who "puppy growls" over food or toys. Presuming you have made the same wise choice, as your puppy grows he may begin more tendencies to vocalize than he displayed at eight or nine weeks old. We affectionately view this as the puppy "finding his voice." For a service animal, vocalizing must be eliminated. The easiest way to do that is from the moment it begins. Correct with a gruff **eh, eh** while you firmly hold the dog's muzzle closed with one hand. When the dog is still and your hand is released, reinforce with **quiet** and praise. Never allow growling noises. Growls in play can quickly turn to growls in earnest. We allow no vocalizing with you and no vocalizing with other animals. As a rule, we do not give a treat or reward any corrected behavior. If you correct a whining dog with this procedure and the moment he is quiet give him a treat, he will learn soon enough to whine, take his correction and get a treat. That is simply setting up a cycle for the dog to repeat unwanted behavior. Instead, once your dog has been corrected for vocalizing, be sure to reinforce with quiet and then move his attention on to an approved task. You could tap your thigh and have the pup walk with you for a step or two, name **heel** for him when he is successful, and then give a treat for that positive behavior.

TEETHING

At approximately sixteen weeks of age, everything your pup has learned so far may begin to fall apart a little. Watch for a change in his ability to focus and pay attention, or for skills you were sure he knew to be less exact. In some cases, perhaps some nipping behaviors will surface or there will be a urination "accident" when your dog had been dry in the house for weeks. Some or all of these things may occur simply because his mouth hurts. Teething is a big event in a dog's life. Can you imagine how you might loose focus if in the span of four to five weeks all of your baby teeth, the whole mouthful, fell out and all your adult sized teeth broke through and grew in?

The best way for you to deal with this big event is with patience and understanding. Teething will end and you will have your old friend back again. Help by supplying the right kind of toys to chew. There are even soft rubber dog toys designed and labeled "for teething puppies" at every pet store. Some are filled with a nontoxic substance to freeze, so that chewing on the cold toy may provide added relief. While this big event is going on, don't give your dog license to forget the rules of the house. Training, naming, housebreaking must all continue.

TOYS

Each of the toys you select for your dog teaches him something. Unfortunately, it's not always something good. We have the "no furniture" rule because it is nearly impossible for the puppy to distinguish between a sofa he may jump on and a chair he may not. There are also rules about toys:

Toys aren't food so they must not be edible. We don't want our dogs filling up on rawhides and pig ears, not only because the nutritional value of those things is questionable, but most importantly because our training tool is the treat we offer for a specific and approved behavior. It is not for lying on the living room floor grinding rawhide bits into the carpet. If the pup is full up on inconsequential snacking his attention will be dimmed to the treats we offer in training.

Toys are given

Toys are given, not taken and shouldn't be left all over the house for the dog to pick and choose. Even an approved toy, or in most households, twenty of them, shouldn't live on the floor for the dog to wander past and decide to engage with.

Clearly, our goal is to have toys available that can be interactive. Tossing a ball or frisbee is great practice for the retrieval skills that are to come. Even an approved rubber or nylon bone should be given for solitary play after your dog has sat in front of you, looked in your eye and you have used the moment to name ***take it*** as the dog's mouth grasps the bone. You will miss out on these great training opportunities by choosing to leave things around the house for the pup to grab at will. A household with dog toys on the floor sends the message that whatever is on the floor is fair game. It would be easy for the puppy to translate that message into toying with shoes, laundry, and at my house, the Sunday newspaper.

Toys that are for dogs are specifically indestructible. No soft stuffed things that can be shredded or unstuffed and may, in fact, look a lot like the cushion on your sofa. No old shoes or socks with knots tied in them, because those things are exactly like your new shoes and your socks without the knots. Do not offer anything with rope fibers to chew and swallow and possibly cause you to spend hundreds of dollars to remove a bowel obstruction. Nothing is used to engage in tug of war, ever.

Balls and other interactive throwing objects are great as are any of a variety of textures and densities of rubber and nylon chew toys. Start small puppies on softer density toys and look for packaging that says "for hard chewers" or "indestructible" if your dog is tough on toys as he grows.

TRAVELING IN THE CAR

Get the puppy used to riding in the car. A service dog will eventually be going everywhere with you. For pet owners, rides in the car to the veterinarian or the park need to be practiced and well tolerated. Use a car harness for your safety while driving and the pup's safety when stopping. A service dog's position in the car is usually next to his partner. If you are driving, your dog is in the front passenger seat. If you are riding in the rear, your dog is beside you. For his comfort, most harnesses allow for your dog to choose either a seated or down position while riding.

COMMON BEHAVIOR MODIFICATIONS

Even the most carefully picked pup, with the most pleasing temperament, may display behaviors you would like to nip in the bud. These same behaviors when displayed by an older animal need to be addressed as a behavior modification project. "The sooner the better," is the rule you must apply. Don't wait for a dog to grow out of a behavior. Address unwanted behaviors with the same method used in all other training. We will identify an unapproved behavior and replace it by training an approved behavior.

NIPPING

Young pups have only their natural instincts to rely on. They come to us as little blank slates on which we will write the parameters of their future behavior. We use the word nipping to describe a very natural tendency for a young puppy to put his mouth on you in a way that brings his teeth in contact with your skin. Nipping is not the word to describe a dog that is actively and/or aggressively biting at you. Never choose to bring home a puppy that is showing aggressive biting behaviors.

Nipping

Puppy nipping is a very natural occurrence because frankly, the pup has only his mouth to use. Left to his own devices, a puppy will use his mouth to lick, chew and nip. Nipping is his natural play time activity. In the cozy litter of puppies you have selected him from, the bunch tumbled and played, nipping at each other. If play became too rough for one of the litter mates, he would give a little yelp to let his brother know to lighten up and take it easy. That yelping noise is what your puppy is waiting to hear from you in testing the distance his play is allowed to go. So yelp! Use a high pitched, rapid fire **ow, ow, ow**. The puppy will release his mouth. Add emphasis, if necessary, by making sure you are very close to your pup's face and by increasing your volume. Repeat the **ow, ow, ow** in a high pitched tone as before.

It is important when teaching your pup not to nip, to have an approved mouth behavior to replace the nipping with. Don't replace nipping with giving toys to chew on or you will be teaching your pup that the way to get a toy is to bite you first. Instead, we encourage "kissing," which replaces the use of teeth with the soft licking of his tongue.

When your puppy kisses you on his own, be sure to name that for him **kisses**. Once your pup has heard your approval and encouragement for the kissing behavior, you can then use it to redirect any nipping he may do. First the correction **ow, ow, ow** and when he releases, redirect his behavior by asking for kisses. Most puppies will mimic kissing you with their tongue if you will get close to the pup's face and flick your own tongue in and out of your mouth rapidly.

BARKING

Most young pups don't do a lot of barking. Avoid selecting a puppy that is very vocal with whining or barking. As your puppy grows and begins to discover his voice, name and reward quiet moments with **quiet**. You can correct small annoyance noise with **eh, eh, eh** and then naming **quiet** when the puppy settles. Any attention-seeking barks should be immediately halted by grasping the dog's muzzle and once he is still, naming that moment **quiet**. Again, be sure to reinforce quiet moments with **quiet**—never take your dog out of his kennel in response to barking, or let him go outside in response to his barking. Be clear that nothing good ever happens because of barking. It is the strength of your reprimand that will startle and quiet the pup.

With a dog showing signs of a more chronic barking problem the resolution has to be a more startling experience for the dog. We don't want to encourage a lot of interaction with a barking animal, much in the same way we don't want to give attention to any disapproved behaviors. The correction must seem to not come from you, in that you don't want to be reinforcing that his barking will gain your attention. Rather, you must initiate a correction that will seem to be a direct consequence of the barking he is doing.

Loud and harmless is what we are looking for. It is the strength of this reprimand that will startle and quiet the pup. Particularly successful are pots dropped on the floor or a metal pie plate thrown against the kennel door. Keep in mind, these are not solutions to be used with tiny puppies. Do your homework and don't bring home a whiny or barking pup. Use **quiet** as the name for moments of quiet. Don't use the word when the dog is barking or you will be naming his noisy behavior rather than his stillness.

PAWING FOR ATTENTION

Attention seeking behaviors, such as pawing or nudging

Pawing

you for petting, need to be discouraged. The best way is to take stock of your own behavior and make sure the pup is getting plenty of good positive attention for doing the things we ask him to do. Particularly important is remembering our rule of *no affection or attention unless the puppy is sitting or lying down.* You can go crazy with love and attention when he is doing those things. If he should paw at you for attention, simply turn away. If you are sitting when he exhibits pawing behavior, stand up and turn away. This problem will resolve if you are firm in your commitment to only reward the behaviors you want to see continue.

PAWING / DIGGING

I love to tell this story, so please indulge me. I once had a client who called me in a panic, sobbing that she had to get rid of her new Beagle puppy because it had just eaten her sofa. "Eaten your sofa!" I exclaimed, "how could that be?" "No, really", she assured me, "there is a hole, six full inches in diameter at the lower right front corner of my sofa and all the stuffing has been pulled out!"

"Who was watching the puppy today?" I asked.

Her 15 year old son had been home all day with the puppy, in the same room with the puppy. She was certain of this because the family computer was in that room and her son had been doing homework.

"Ahhhh, homework," I replied.

Doing homework doesn't mean you're watching the puppy. Being in the same room doesn't mean you're watching the puppy. **Only watching the puppy means you're watching the puppy.**

Licking the corner of the sofa was certainly the puppy's bad—but correctable—behavior. Everything that happened after that was simply not his fault. So if your pup is chewing the furniture, digging holes in the back yard, or any other progressively destructive behavior, only the first lick or paw in the dirt is his fault. The rest, I am afraid, is yours.

SOLITARY DESTRUCTION

When the puppy is to be left alone we have a safe and secure place where the puppy is trained to find comfort and calm. It is his kennel. Use it.

SPECIAL NOTES

Some of the behaviors we must learn to modify are going to be yours, not the puppy's. Start by "puppy proofing" your home much like you would for a toddler. All toxins and cleaning supplies, all small objects that could be chewed or swallowed, must be safely away. Make sure you have a travel crate or safety harness for your dog in the car. A quick stop in a moving auto can send a puppy flying like a missile.

If you have very small children in your home their interactions with the puppy must be monitored. No nose to nose contact until the puppy is past the teething phase and has been kid proofed with your "OW" training. Allow petting only from the neck back toward the tail, not near the head, while puppy nipping is an issue.

Children's game playing should not encourage the puppy to chase or jump. If the puppy gets revved up to running and jumping , teach the child to stop and stand still, "be a tree" and turn away from the pup until he settles down. Ask your child to use his lowest, "basement," voice tones. Low tones make dogs calm.

For many, the most difficult adjustment to make is not engaging in conversations with your animal. It is the one single training component you are completely in control of. I have often been told by pet owners that they chat to their animal because, "Really, he understands me." Please believe me when I tell you that your cute pup, cocking his head to one side with an amusing look on his face in response to your comment, "What do you think?" is simply thinking, "What in the world does she want me to do?"

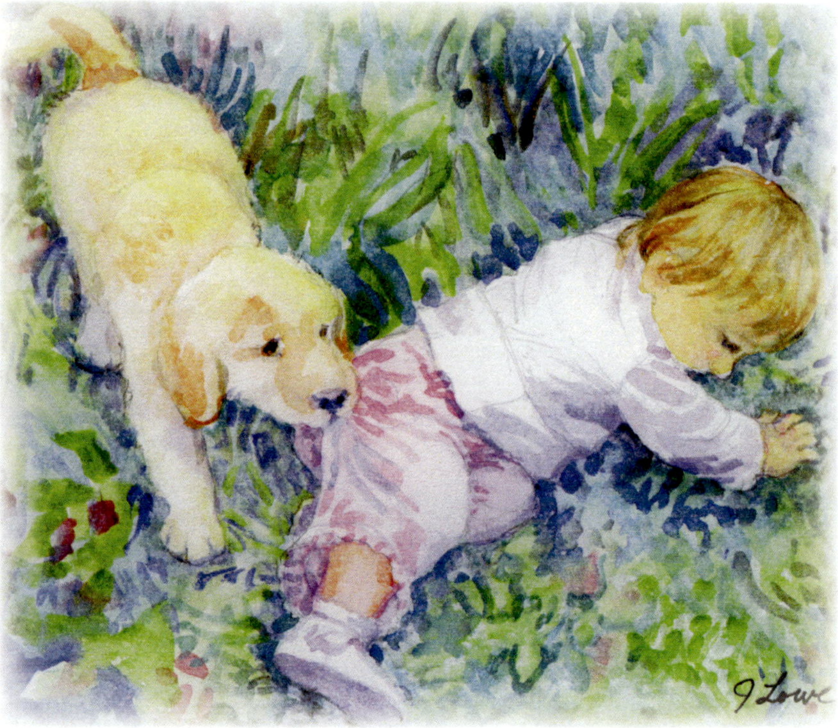

COMMANDS

After several weeks of naming the behaviors your puppy is naturally engaging in, you will clearly see that his recognition of the word you are using is beginning to form. If every time his bottom hits the floor you are paying attention and say *sit*, he quickly will grow to learn what that sound means. Take time to read ahead through all the words we use and the behaviors we need to name to be able to call on them later as commands.

Command words are the exact same words we have used to name the dog's behavior, exactly the same. The change is that now we will ask the dog to perform the behavior "on command." We aren't going to wait for our puppy to sit down and name the behavior for him. We are going to ask him to *sit* and expect that enough naming and recognition has occurred for him to understand and perform what we ask.

Command words are spoken clearly, firmly and with a moderate volume of voice. There is no yelling and no repetition of the command word. Be close to your dog and have good attention from him before you begin. Once the command word is spoken, wait in stillness and silence and give the dog an opportunity to perform what has been directed. When successful, he gets a treat and praise. If he is not successful, repeat the command word once as you physically assist in positioning him in the proper position you have commanded and give the treat and praise once he is successful. If after a time or two the dog will not respond to the command word without some additional intervention on your part, then he clearly has no recognition of the word you are using. That, I am afraid, is your fault and not his. Name every time and all the time each of the things we want to instill as approved and desirable behaviors.

You begin now with instruction on commanding all of the basic behaviors any dog can master. Command words have been paired with the hand signs we use to indicate the behavior asked for. For service work, we train both hand and vocal commands at the same time and eventually use them interchangeably as the situation calls for.

THE BEGINNING COMMANDS

1. **Come**... has been named every time the dog walks toward you...Hand sign is open palms facing the dog at

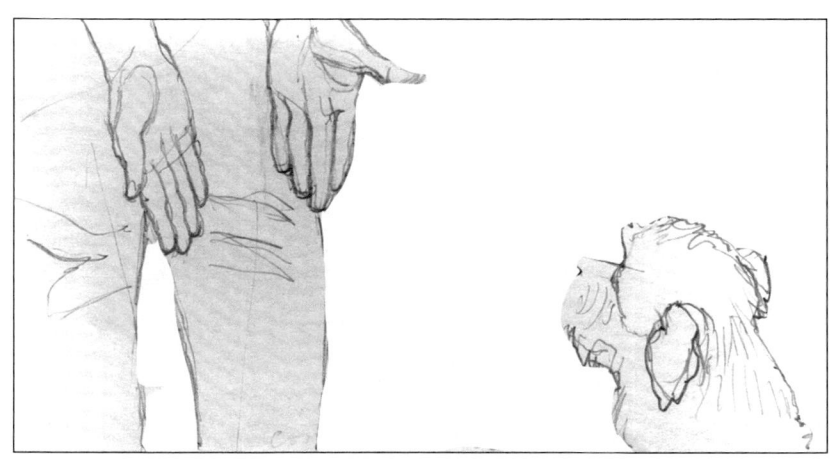

Come

your knee to waist level . Do not attach the training of *come* to any negative outcome. Don't call your dog to *come* and then put him directly into his crate and leave him alone for three hours. *Come* must always be associated with the best treat and the most enthusiastic praise. If you use *come* to mean "your fun is over" or "you're in trouble now," you will ruin the command response.

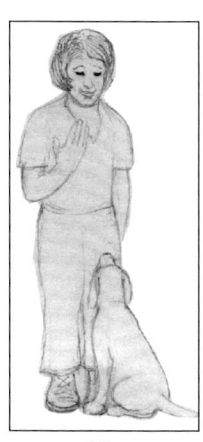

2. **Sit**... has been named every time the dog sits. The hand signal is one arm bent upright at elbow with your palm facing toward you. Sitting is now a requirement for doors opening, at the completion of a *come* command, giving your dog food at his mealtimes, and all treats.

Sit

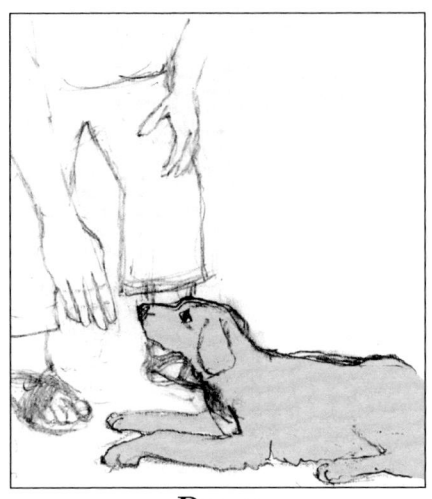

Down

3. **Down**... has been named for all down postures. The hand signal is one hand, fingers together, palm facing floor, moving toward the floor in one rapid movement. ***Down*** is now a requirement for the dog during your meals, while you are watching TV, working at your computer, whenever you are engaged in a sedentary activity. If the dog's position is confined to under a desk or table, name that ***under*** as you lead your dog into position and command ***down***.

4. **Go to work**.... is the naming of placing your dog's service coat on and the rules for behavior while wearing it. The service coat must indicate a heightened expectation of performance by the dog. He must sit or stand quietly while it is placed on. You may hold a treat as a lure at the opening of the coat so the dog learns to place his head through the collar. While in the coat no one may approach, touch or otherwise distract the dog's attention from his training work. For pet owners, a service coat will not be worn. You may take this command to address the leashing of your dog. Always begin with your dog in a controlled, sitting position.

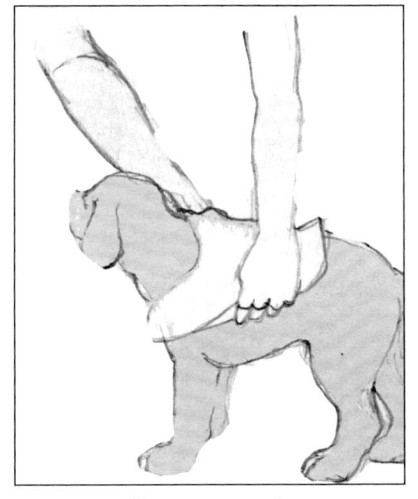

Go to work

5. **Look**.... remember to use the *look* command as a transition between any two or more instructions you ask your dog to follow. If your intention is to call your dog to come, sit in front of you and then lie down, take a moment to draw your dog's attention to your eyes by moving your index finger from in front of his nose up to your own nose between commands. We want to instill the habit of your dog looking to you to find out what it is you would like him to do next.

Look

Dogs Don't Speak English

GAINING CONTROL

1. **Heeling with Sit...** The dog must now learn to come to a sit position at your left side whenever you choose to stop your forward walking motion. This will include all intersections and crosswalks, stopping for bicycles, baby carriages and the like, as well as stops chosen at random for behavior practice and reinforcement. Begin by giving the *sit* command each time you stop forward motion, and reward your dog. At each stop, gradually lengthen the time before you give the sit command. Give your dog an auditory clue that you are about to come to a stop by shuffling your feet the last few steps. Try to stand in silence a moment until the dog sits on his own each time you come to a stop.

Heeling with Sit

2. **Stay....** The dog must remain still, usually either in a sitting or down position, until released by the words **"O.K."** The hand signal is a closed fingered palm facing the dog at his nose level. Begin this sequence at mealtime as the food dish will provide enormous incentive for success. Before placing the dog's dish down for feeding, grasp the back of his collar

Stay

firmly in your left hand. Your restraint will simulate for him a still restrained or *stay* position. Hold him firmly in that position, place the food dish down with your right hand and immediately place your right palm in front of and touching his nose. Name this position *stay*, immediately say *O.K., eat* and release his collar so he may eat. The exercise continues at each meal time progressing to less grasping of his collar, until only the palm touching his nose is necessary. Progress from there must continue until the palm and word indicating *stay* may be done while you are standing erect and separate from the dog. The final exercise will be to put the dog in a *sit*, *stay* away from his food dish area while you are preparing and placing his food dish down. At any point, as these exercises progress, if your dog breaks his *stay* position, you will stop the exercise by not continuing to fill his dish or by picking the dish up from the floor. Return the dog to the exercise and *stay* command and start again until he waits for your release word *O.K., eat* to move from the *stay*. *Stay* exercises should also be incorporated into commands for all *sit* or *down* activities you are currently using, particularly at open doors, *sit*, *stay*; while you are eating, *down*, *stay*; and on his mat, *place*, *stay*.

    3. **Jump up, Jump off....** This is the named behavior for getting into and out of the car or other equivalent situations. The hand signal is index finger extended with whole arm swinging from low to high across your body for the *up* command and starting from high to low in a swinging motion for *off* command. *Up* is also used as the command for having the animal come up to your chest level with his front paws, while his hind paws are still on the ground. If using a wheelchair, this position will make attaching a leash, collar or coat to your dog much easier. The hand signal is to tap your chest with your hands. Do not engage in practicing the up exercise to your chest unless you are in a seated position. When you are standing, the dog should not be encouraged or taught to jump up. From his up

position when you are seated, *off* is achieved by pointing with your index finger back down toward the ground.

Jump up    **Jump off**

Remember not to confuse the command word *down* in telling your dog to remove himself from something. *Down* only means to lie down on the ground. *Off* means to get off of something or someone.

4. **Lap...** is the name for positioning the dog with his front paws on your lap while his hind quarters remain in a seated position on the ground. For very large dogs, this may be a position better suited to attaching leashes and coats instead of the fully extended body position of tapping your chest for *up*. It is also a very useful position for close body contact and affection given to your dog if sitting or using a

Lap

wheelchair. Practice by having the dog sitting in front of you. While in this position, lift his paws one at a time placing them in your lap. Cover his paws with your hand and while patting them, name the position *lap*. Once this position is learned through naming practice, the hand signal will be patting your lap with one hand.

UPPING THE ANTE

1. **Leave it....** should be named after making a distractive noise, *eh, eh, leave it*, and removal of the offending object or substance. The hand signal is a closed hand, palm facing the dog's nose passing across his face in front of his eyes. *Leave it* is used to indicate the dog may never have the object of interest. It is not a command for something he is likely to be allowed later. The positive

Leave it

reinforcement to a *leave it* command is to command *look*. In this way the dog's attention is immediately redirected towards you and you are able to give a reward for this approved attention. When on leash, the *leave it* may be reinforced by a sharp jerk on the leash. Practice must be done with distractions of an increasingly difficult nature. Remember not to use toys or other approved objects as bait for a *leave it* exercise.

2. **Wait....** will be named when a pause is required in your dog's behavior. The *stay* hand signal is used. *Wait* indicates that the dog may continue at your discretion with your next command. This is particularly useful when passing through narrow areas or at doorways that would not accommodate both you and the dog at your side. It is appropriate in most cases for the dog to *wait* while you

proceed first. You may practice the *wait* exercise with approved toys, as ultimately you will allow your dog to have them. Also practice *wait* at open doors. You want to train your dog not to bolt through without your say so. This is both for safety in getting out of cars, for the odd chance that the front door is left ajar, and for the simple courtesy of having a dog that will wait for your next command.

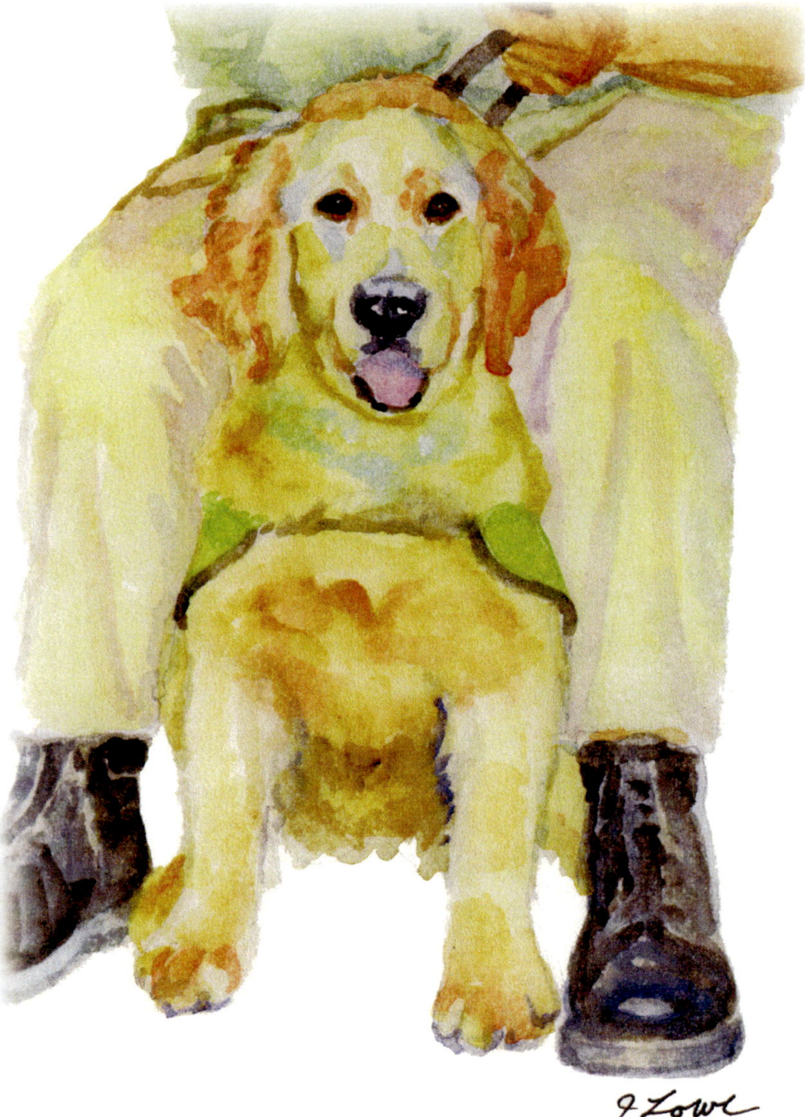
J Lowe

THE KEY TO RETRIEVING

1. **Take it....** has been named each time something is offered to the dog's mouth or the dog has picked something up on his own. The hand sign is forearm parallel to the floor in front of your body with an open hand, palm facing the floor. The hand closes and moves back towards the body as if pulling. As soon as the ***take it*** command is regularly responded to with a training object such as a toy, additional objects of different materials are to be practiced. If the object is one that will be used often as part of service work, the object to be put in the dog's mouth should be named as the first part of the command, ***pen, take it, key, take it.*** Objects are taught first from the hand, next from the floor, and lastly from other locations such as from tables or items left on chairs or stair steps. Working with plastic and rubber objects should come first. Next, move to wood and paper objects which must be delivered to you without excessive mouthing and wetness. Lastly, work on metal objects such as keys. These can be the most difficult because of their particular mouth feel to the dog.

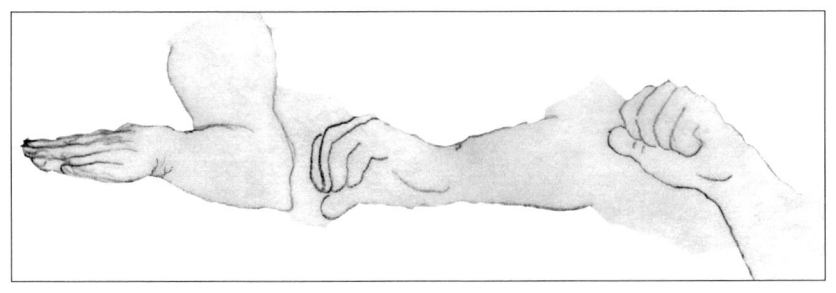

→ → **Take it** → →

2. **Hold it.....** has been named each time an object is in the dog's mouth as a held object not as a chew toy. The hand sign is a closed fist held perpendicular to the floor. You should start with the closed fist just touching the dog's muzzle so he is not able to release the object. Practice should continue until the command can be given in a standing position apart from your dog.

Hold it

3. **Drop it...** has been named each time the dog has released an object from his mouth to the floor. The hand sign is a close fisted hand opening with palm to the floor

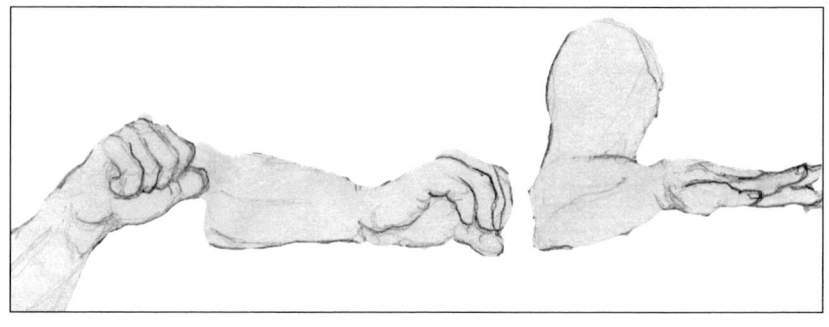

→ → **Drop it** → →

as if dropping something. If there has not been sufficient opportunity to name this behavior, lure your dog into dropping an object, like a toy, onto the floor by flicking it out of his mouth with your hand.

A finger or two placed behind the object in your dog's mouth and pushing it rapidly forward and out , will give you the training moment to name ***drop it*** as the object hits the floor. Do not pull the object out of your dog's mouth from the front. That action resembles a tug of war game and is never allowed.

4. **Give it...** has been named each time the dog has released something into your hand or you have removed something from the dog's mouth with your hand. The

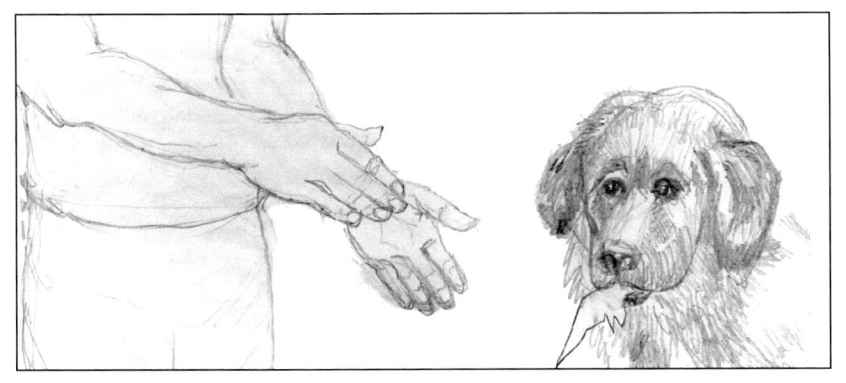

Give it

hand sign is an open flat palmed hand facing upward under the dog's mouth as if waiting for something to be placed in it. Rewards may only be given when an object is released in the hand without having to stretch or reach for it. Help your dog have initial success by placing your receiving hand under his mouth. Proceed to more difficulty with your hand apart from your dog and closer to your own body. ***Give it*** means in your hand. You may point to your open hand to help indicate where you want the object placed during initial training. Eventually, the open hand alone must indicate ***give it***. The object is to be named first as skills progress.

5. **Bring it...** has been named each time the dog carries anything toward you. The hand sign is the same as ***come***. An especially good exercise to practice ***bring it*** is with two people challenging the dog to ***bring*** an object back and forth between them with a ***take it*** and ***give it*** command from each person in turn and a treat at each rotation.

Dogs Don't Speak English

BODY POSITIONS

1. **Finish...** This change in the dog's body position must be initially practiced by luring the dog with a treat

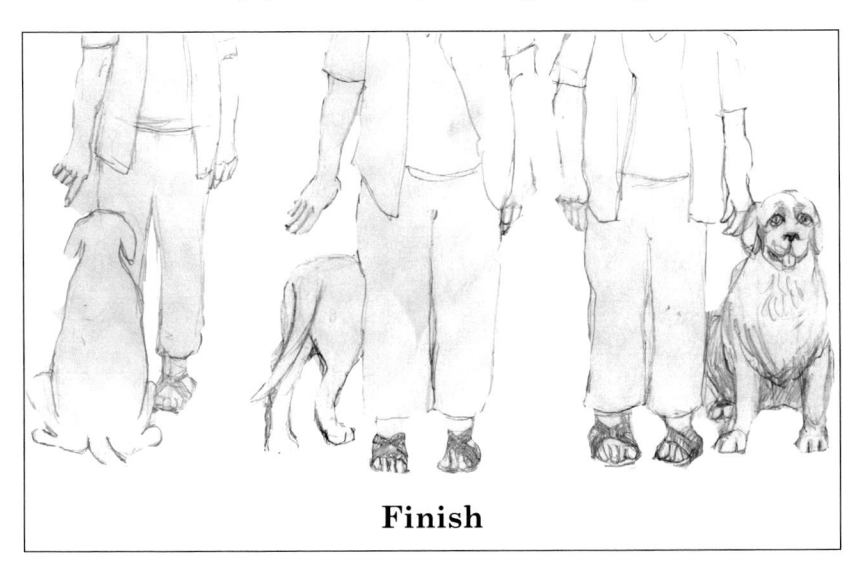

Finish

and naming the behavior for him. It is unlikely that this body movement will occur on a regular basis until it has been taught. The goal is to command a dog from whatever he is doing to sit at your left side ready to engage in the next command activity. The exercise begins with the dog sitting in front of you, looking at you. Hold a treat in your right hand and lure the dog around the back of your body, changing the treat over to your left hand at the midway point. Do not release the treat to the dog until he has come to a sitting position at your left side. As you release the treat, name the exercise *finish*. Repeat the exercise until the command can be given without the lure of the treat. The hand sign is an extended index finger pointed from the front of your body around to the right as if sending the dog around you as you say *finish*.

2. **Stand...** This is another exercise that begins with a lure in order to name a behavior. With the dog in a *sitting* or *down* position, hold a treat just at the end of

Stand

his nose and pull the treat forward. As the dog rises to follow the treat name the behavior *stand* and release the treat. It is important to pull the treat *straight out* in front of the dog and *not up*. You don't want to encourage the dog to jump for the treat, simply to follow it forward into a standing position. Practice from both a sitting and down start. The hand sign is moving your hand from the dog's nose straight back toward yourself, as if you were pulling him with a string.

3. **Variations of Stay...** Increasing controlled stay positions is very important. The first exercise is to put your dog in a *down, stay* position and be able to walk completely around his position in a circle without the dog rising or moving his body position to see where you are. He may turn his head, but not move his position by readjusting, or swimming around on the floor. He must remain in a *stay* as you "disappear" out of his field of vision.

The second exercise is to incorporate long and longer periods of time in which the dog will maintain his stay. The rule of thumb in this training is to increase the time twice and decrease it once. For example, 1 minute, $1^{1/2}$ minutes, 30 seconds; then 1 minute, 2 minutes, 1 minute; $1^{1/2}$ minutes, 3 minutes, 1 minute, and so on. We always plan training difficulty with a harder, harder, easier pattern.

The third exercise deals with the stay position held at

some distance from you. Start the exercise with ***down, stay*** and take two steps backward while facing the dog. The dog is then released with ***O.K., come*** and rewarded with a treat. This exercise continues until greater distance can be maintained while you back up from the dog and then with you turning and walking away from the dog. Be sure to go back to working on smaller distances once you increase the distraction of turning and walking away. For all these exercises, work from starting positions of ***down, stay; sit, stay*** and ***stand, stay***.

  4. **Position Practice** . . . When we examine Body Positioning , we are really talking about having our dog

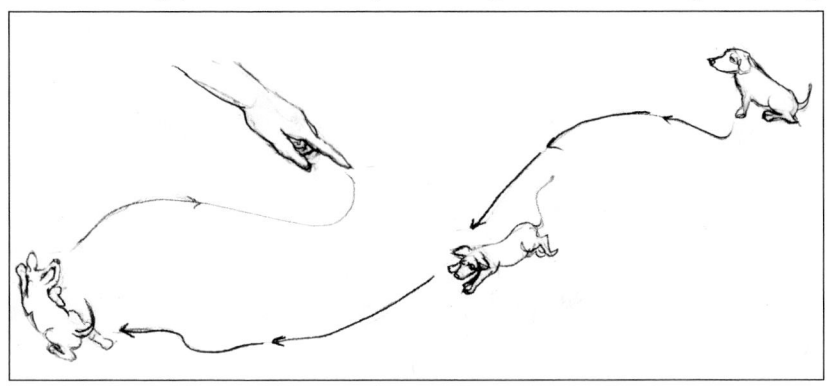

Position Practice

where we want him to be in relation to ourselves. We began teaching this "where to be" philosophy by pointing our index finger to a spot called ***place*** and by using our finger to indicate ***jump off***. I encourage you to practice more variations of positioning by using your index finger in an excercise we call ***Doodling***. Much like doodling random lines on paper with a pencil, we use our index finger to draw imaginery lines as we point to the floor and encourage our dog to follow. You can start with your finger as close to the floor as necessary, even tapping a random spot and treating your dog when he hits the spot you have indicated. Practice by moving away from direct contact with the floor and simply pointing to a spot. Next, point at three or more spots in succession before treating. Eventually, you will be able to draw your imaginary lines on the floor and have your dog follow your direction wherever you point.

MORE BODY POSITIONS

1. **Side...** This exercise positions the dog to the right side. It is the opposite of the heel position. Practice walking in corridors and staircases, holding the leash to position the dog on your right and name this position *side*. The hand sign is tapping your right thigh with your hand. This sign may also be used as encouragement and reinforcement during training. Be sure to step out with your right foot first to encourage the dog to move with you at your right side. When the dog marks this position correctly, immediately name and treat. Be sure to incorporate some time in left side or *heel* training during each session so that the dog identifies both positions.

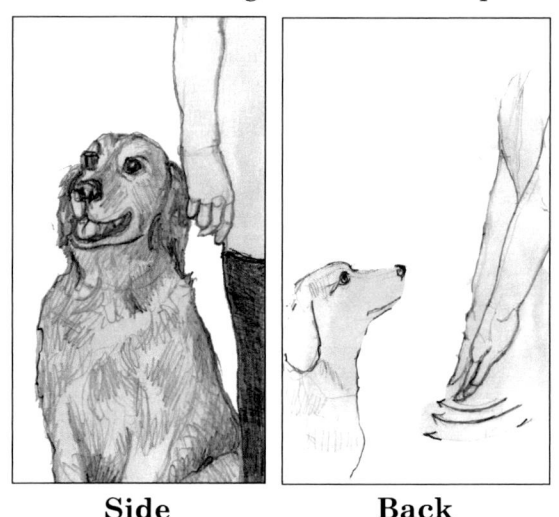

Side   **Back**

2. **Back...** You will need to create a narrow walkway, large enough for the dog to move forward and backward, yet not wide enough for the dog to turn around. A coffee table pushed close to the edge of a sofa or chairs lined up to reduce the width of a hallway will work. With the dog

in front of you in one of these confined areas, take a step toward the dog and as he steps backward to avoid being stepped on say **back**. Keep slowly walking toward the dog and repeating the name of this behavior, **back**. The hand sign is open hand, back of the hand facing the dog and a waving motion as if to shoo the dog backward.

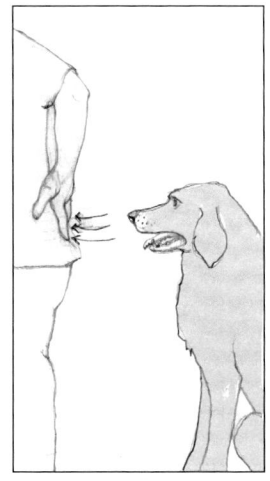

Follow

3. **Follow...** The same narrow corridor of space is needed to practice having the dog follow behind you instead of walking along with you on your right or left side. The hand sign is tapping the small of your back as you move forward with the dog following behind. You may begin working on this position with the dog on a monk leash short enough to insure his body position stays to your rear. If the available walking space is narrow enough, just positioning yourself as the leader should be enough.

Dogs Don't Speak English

GOING THE DISTANCE

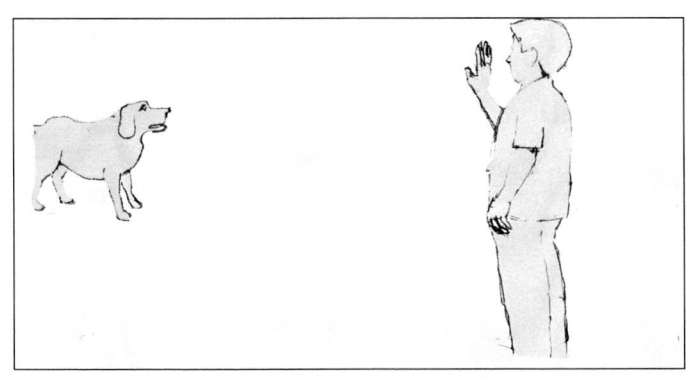

Distance Commands

1. **Distance Commands...** Of the skills already learned it is important to continue working toward obedience at greater and greater distances away from you. If a car comes careening around a corner out of nowhere, your dog's ability to obey your commands at any distance can save your dog's life. Practice with hand signals alone, words alone, and both combined. If from a distance the dog has a tendency to move toward you as you give a command you can break him of this by first raising your hand in the *stay* sign. Follow this with the next command sign, as for *sit*. If the dog moves forward toward you instead of directly into the sit position, immediately repeat the sign for *stay* while taking one loud stomping footstep towards him. Make sure you begin work on distance commands at a close enough distance to be successful. We start from a point of success and then, as with all increased levels of distraction, make the same exercise more difficult once, more difficult twice, and then back to an easier level. You don't want to continue to up the difficulty with no end in sight or the dog may lose his ability to focus. He will be made to feel that nothing is ever enough to please you. Our goal is always to keep him challenged and happy in his work.

2. **Go Commands...** These are commands that create distance between you and the dog by your command to send him away from you. Practice sending him to his kennel from greater distances by attaching *go* before the command *kennel in*. Attach *go* from a distance before *place*; before taking objects *go, pen, take it*. The hand sign for all go commands is pointing while moving the hand in the direction your dog should attend to.

Go Commands

THINGS TO KNOW

Once you have accomplished reliable compliance to these commands we are able to proceed with specific skill training. Those are the remarkable abilities service dogs display by opening doors, drawers and the refrigerator. These animals retrieve dropped objects and bring the ringing telephone to someone in a bed or using a wheelchair. We train hitting light switches, wheelchair heeling and other skills specific to the individual needs of the placement partner these animals join.

As we continue with our next sections of intermediate and advanced skills, please keep in mind that we train animals to perform tasks not tricks. These are work related goals. If your interest as a personal pet owner is to have your dog roll over or to balance a dog biscuit on his nose, we do not address those specifics. Whether teaching a trick or a task, the method is the same.

If you are continuing on as a service dog trainer, it is now we strongly suggest adding the dressing of your dog in an identifying service dog coat. Many types are readily available online. Look for those that are simple to dress and adjust with single straps and Velcro rather than buckles. Later on you may want to invest in more costly harness apparatus for brace work or packs for toting personal items. We suggest dressing, because the dogs clearly begin to understand this as a call to attention.

It marks the moment of requiring a heightened sense of attention to task. As we dress the dog we name **go to work** and the coat is fastened. In addition, your dog, when working, must attend only to you. The wearing of a service coat will, hopefully, dissuade passersby from approaching or engaging your working animal. If you cannot find a coat or afford one, cut a large square of fabric as a bandana and use the tying on of this bandana to mark the moment **go to work**. Make sure to remove the bandana as you would remove the service coat when the dog is not "on duty."

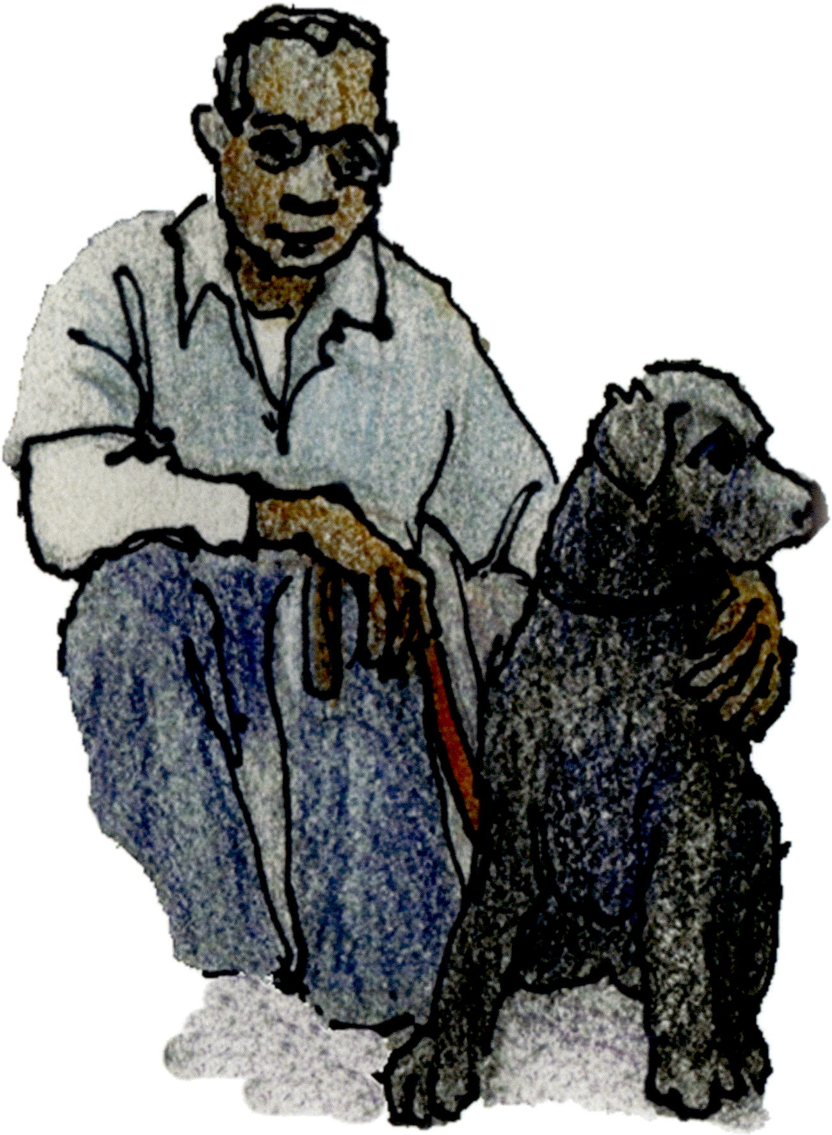

INTERMEDIATE TRAINING

Please remember not to race through the basic training. This isn't a contest to see how fast the animal can acquire new skills. Rather, it is far more important to do fewer skills really well. We are looking for a command response that is consistent and immediate, "first time, every time." Better still is a dog whose behavior is so conditioned that no command need be given at all. Our dogs sit in front of doors without being asked because they know through repetition that the door will not open for them to go outside until they sit.

In most cases, service dog training takes two years before a partner placement is made. You will do a disservice to the process by forcing the issue of acquiring more skills if they are all done badly. "Almost" doesn't count. Move slowly through the training process and give praise and treats only when they are earned.

Intermediate training addresses behavior (how the dog acts) and skills (what tasks the dog performs). It is important to alternate exercises and build competence in both areas at the same time. You want the dog to understand both features equally. A dog able to pick a coin up off the floor and bring it to you is remarkably skilled. If this dog won't come to you when called, all his other skills pale in comparison. All through this learning process it is important to continue to go back and work through your beginning skills. Keep those exercises current in your dog's mind with practice, practice, practice.

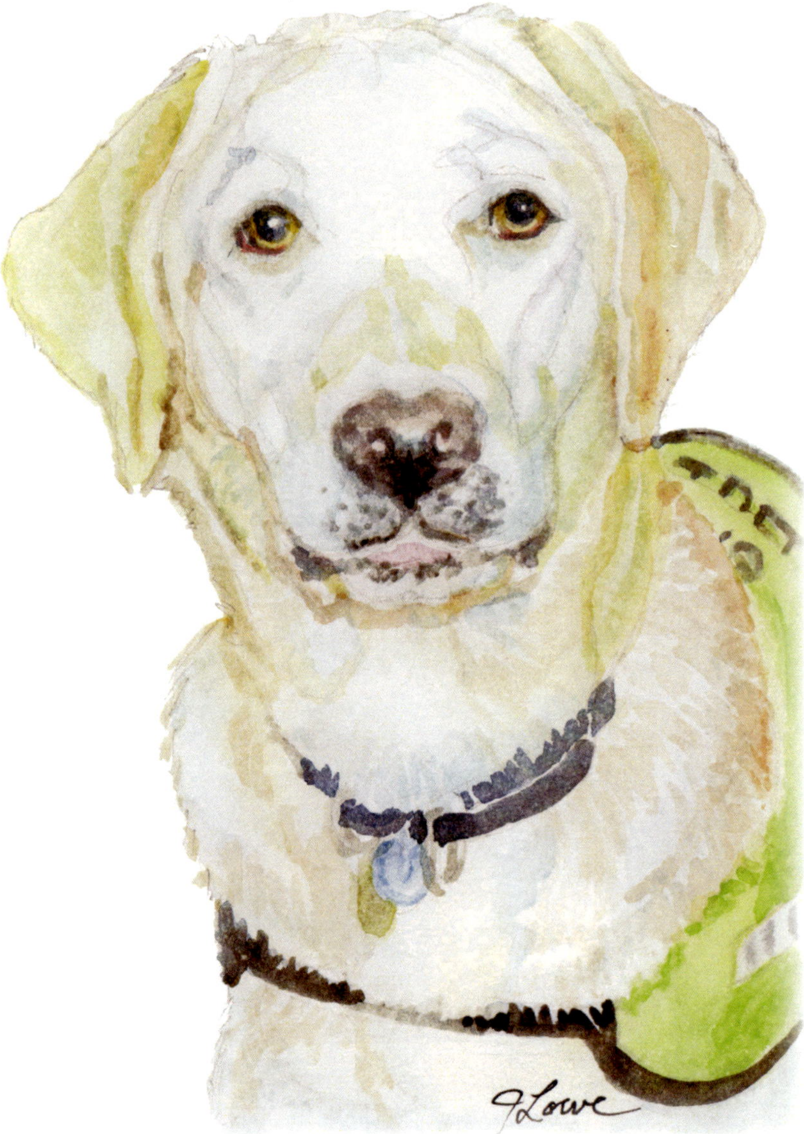

WORKING OFF LEASH

This skill is rooted in all the work you did to heel train your new pup. Remember walking through your house, tapping your thigh, encouraging your dog to stay close and walk beside you before he had a clue what a leash was for? We're about to do it again. The goal is to have a dog that understands his place is with you unless, at your discretion, he is told to *stay* or *go* somewhere you direct.

Begin by forming a habit in your home to tap your thigh and say *heel* each time you get up to move anywhere. As an exercise, try placing two chairs at some distance from each other and move in a figure eight pattern around them. Lots of thigh tapping and *heel* encouragement should be employed when your dog is on the outside curve of the figure eight. When he is at the inside curve simply move closer toward his body and continue to move. In a secure fenced area, practice these same behaviors. The out of doors will offer more distractions of sights and smells. Continue to work toward keeping his attention with the *look* command as needed. Alternate your pace from fast to slow to a jog. Alternating your pace is an excellent exercise for leashed practice as well. Stop your movement at intervals and expect your dog to sit at your side. Try to find alternate, safely fenced areas for practice. Try to provide spaces where your dog is not specifically aware of his boundaries and restrictions. This will make his attention toward you, or lack of it, more telling.

Once his attention is reliable, practice an off leash exercise that you can duplicate frequently. We generally use going from the house to the car. Begin with the dog on a ten foot or longer leash, naming the activity *go to the car* in your higher pitched, enthusiastic voice. We want the leash to offer no resistance or feeling of confinement to the dog. It is only used as a safeguard until the behavior is perfected. First, you may offer a treat when the dog is seated outside the car door waiting for your command to ***jump in***. Work toward offering the treat only after the dog has successfully entered his designated seat. As reliability progresses, you may add other off leash tasks such as going to get the mail.

All the while, remember to encourage the dog to follow your steps inside the house and out. Where you go, he goes. That's his job.

STAIRS

In any household, a dog racing up the stairs ahead of you or tripping you as he flies down the stairs from behind can cause annoyance and even injury. We need to practice a safe habit of positioning your dog.

Waiting

Waiting For You

In most cases, we recommend training the dog to wait for you to pass first, either up or down the staircase. Once you have reached your destination, then call your waiting dog to come to you. Maintaining your position of leadership and command means *you go first*. All the lessons your dog already has learned in reliably sitting and waiting make this exercise possible.

Simply put your dog in a ***sit***, ***wait*** at the bottom of a staircase and after you have climbed, turn to face your dog and call him to *come*. Remember to stand back a bit from the edge of the staircase so that the dog has room to position himself in a sit in front of you when he reaches the top. Command *finish*, which will position him to your left side and then tap your thigh with the command *heel* and continue your movement. As you practice you may eliminate treating until the completion of *finish*.

The exercise duplicates itself in the reverse, with you commanding *sit*, *wait* for your dog at the top of a staircase as you descend first. This is sometimes slightly harder for the dog, as his head weight and enthusiasm makes it more difficult to control the speed of his descent. Practice this exercise by stepping back from the last step so you don't get plowed into and make sure that coming to a full stop and sitting in front of you is the successful completion of the descent. Continue with *finish* and *heel* as before.

For dogs that seem to barrel up and, particularly, down a staircase, you must practice moderating their speed. This is done on a leash and will be outlined as we discuss exercises for "Bracing on stairs."

Going Ahead

As an alternative to commanding your dog to wait for you either at the top or bottom of staircases, you may want to send your dog ahead. This is accomplished by sending the dog, *go,* up or down the stairs and indicating where by swinging your arm and pointing with your index finger. Once he has reached your desired destination, be sure to command *sit*, *wait*. He should remain still and well positioned as you go to meet him. The dog should receive a treat when you reach him. Depending on his position you would then command *heel* and continue your movement or first require *finish* to better ready him on your left side.

Bracing

Bracing refers to using your animal as an aid to support your own movement. Sometimes it is simply having the dog remain in a still and stable standing position in front of you so that you may lean on him to support you in rising from a chair or steady you as you walk down a hallway. This steadying feature would certainly depend on the size and weight of both you and your dog. In addition, the dog's conformation and soundness must be evaluated before you do damage to him by applying too much weight or pressure and you must learn the appropriate positioning of your hands on his shoulders and hips. For reliable guidance your veterinarian will likely want to x-ray and evaluate your particular dog before you brace your body weight on his.

Brace

The brace position is an excellent aid in mobility readiness even if no weight is applied to the animal. It is particularly useful on open staircases or when no railing is provided. The dog is taught to walk one step at a time, both up and down a staircase at a pace moderated to your own. We begin practice going up a staircase.

With no leash attached to your dog's collar, stand at the bottom of an indoor staircase with the dog to your left in a heel position. Grasp his collar in your left hand. (If your dog is too small in comparison to your height when standing for you to comfortably grasp his collar, then he is not a candidate for brace work of any kind. You may work toward pacing his movement on stairs, if you choose, by working these exercises with his leash attached.)

Continue to hold the collar throughout this exercise. Step firmly, left foot then right, placing both your feet together on the first step and name the position **brace**. Repeat this movement and naming **brace** on to the second step. This time encourage your dog to put his front feet up on the step with you by applying some control to his collar. Repeat this process, one step at a time, controlling the dog's movement by forward pressure on his collar as needed and naming each step **brace**. You must also control the dog by pressure on his collar to prevent him from taking more than one step at a time.

Ten to fifteen steps is quite enough for the first time. When you get to the top be sure to reward him with a treat and your vocal enthusiasm. Then command your dog **sit**, **wait** and after you have descended the staircase, call him to you and repeat the exercise going up the stairs. This is a tiring exercise for your dog because it requires a great deal of muscle control on his part. A few repetitions of the exercise are enough for the first time. You are looking to get increasingly better response with less physical control of his collar and fewer verbal repetitions of your naming word **brace**. Do not begin working on the brace technique down a staircase until very good recognition has developed going up. The goal is to place your hand across your dog's shoulder, say the command word **brace** and have him move with you, at your pace, up the stairs.

As soon as you no longer need to apply collar control for upward bracing you may begin work descending the stairs. Begin on a short staircase of six steps or less or at the lower end of any staircase with only a few steps in front of you. The dog is positioned on the left and his collar is grasped firmly. Understand that as you proceed forward, gravity and the dog's head weight will encourage him to move forward. Keep hold of his collar, limiting his ability to move more than one step at a time with you and name ***brace***. The exercise continues as before adding more steps to the downward process as control is improved. If you are patient and wait to begin training the descent on stairs until the dog understands the brace concept from his practice going up a staircase, you will have much better results.

Finally, be sure to practice with your dog on both your left and right sides once he has mastered both directions. He must be ready to assist you according to the need of the situation. When practicing with your dog to the right, be sure to encourage his learning by stepping out first with your right foot. You may also incorporate brace command practice while walking on flat surfaces.

Tap your thigh on the side you would like your dog to assist you. Say the command ***brace*** and hold out your hand on that side with your palm facing toward the floor. Your dog will learn to move with you, under the hand you have indicated, while you rest your hand on his shoulder. If brace work is a function of the service your dog will provide be sure to invest in a good quality rigid-handled harness. Readily available from on-line sources, the harness will allow better control of your dog with less pressure on his shoulders and spine.

TUG

From the very first pages, you will find our directive, ***never engage in tug of war games*** with your dog. Now we will tell you why. Tug is a very specific activity and command word we will use to direct your animal in service. Tug is the beginning of a compound command that will enable your animal to open doors, drawers and the refrigerator.

Tug

We begin by introducing a tug strap to the dog. A tug strap can be made of any resilient material such as leather, rope or as we use in training, the handle end of old nylon dog leashes. The handle end refers to the loop of a leash you would hold while walking your dog, and from the end of that loop we need about 10 to 12 inches more of the leash. We cut off and discard the rest.

Just as we introduced objects to the dog's mouth in earlier exercises of ***take it***, we want the dog to take the leash end in his mouth while we hold on to the loop. While sitting in front of your dog, hold the leash end up to the dog and use the command words ***take it***. Treat and praise your dog for success. Once the dog will reliably take and hold the strap, give some slight pulling tension from the loop end you are holding and name this *tug*. Practice this tension on the strap and naming of *tug* until the dog begins to tug on the strap himself. The tension on the strap should be coming from the dog's mouth not from your hand. Your hold is the immovable fixed point. The dog is exerting the force. Name this *tug* and remove the strap from his mouth by offering a treat and praise, *tug*.

   The next step is to hold the loop end of the strap in your hand while standing, with the leash end hanging vertically downward. Use the command words *take it, tug*. Praise and treat success.

As soon as these exercises have accomplished our goal of the tug being initiated by the dog's mouth and not your hand, we must proceed carefully. This is *not* a game. Refrain from tugging back on the strap. As soon as you feel tension on the strap from the dog offer the treat immediately so he will be encouraged to release and take the treat. We don't want to see any side to side head shaking while the dog is engaged in tugging and certainly *no* vocalizing from the dog. Time your offering of the treat quickly to eliminate any chance for game playing. If there is any hesitation to release the strap for the treat that is being offered, then use your command words *give it*. Be sure to put the strap away when not training and continue to abstain from all tug of war games with toys.

HIT AND TOUCH

Mobility service animals may give assistance to persons confined to bed or using a wheelchair. Training addresses the specifics of the animal to touch, hit or press buttons, bells or even emergency call apparatus when an individual cannot. For pet owners, the first steps toward hit commands will teach your dog to put his paw into your hand. If that is your only interest, you may name this exercise **give paw, slap five** or anything else you choose. Our interest is to produce an animal that will learn to do much more with the pressure of his foot.

Hit

Exactly as we have shown and named behaviors for all of our training, we begin by showing our dog what **hit** is. Begin by commanding your dog to **sit** and then come down to his level, sitting on the floor facing him. Extend your hand toward your dog with palm up and with that hand, in a single motion, lift your dog's front paw off the ground with your outstretched hand, raising it to his chest level. As his paw comes to rest in your open palm, name this **hit**. Give him a treat as you say **hit**. Let his foot drop and repeat this process eight or ten times. Do not rush.

Let the recognition begin to develop that *hit* is the name of his paw in your hand. Next, hold out the hand you had been using to lift your dog's paw and let it remain open, palm upward, at his chest level while you use your other hand to place the paw into that waiting palm. Name this *hit* and give a treat.

This is repeated, without rushing, another six or eight times. Finally, hold out that same hand, palm upward, at your dog's chest level and wait, quietly. You may do a slight up and down movement of your open hand if you need to indicate more clearly what you want your dog to do. You may even use your other hand to gently nudge the dog's foot from behind. Do be patient and allow the dog to initiate the placing of his paw into your palm. If it does not happen, go back and begin the exercises again. This is generally a process that works in just a time or two. When your dog does initiate the correct placement of his paw be sure to name it *hit* and treat him. Have him do the exercise on his own a few more times, with you doing nothing more than sitting quietly and waiting with your palm extended. Once this is accomplished, you can hold out your hand, use the command word *hit* and expect the dog to place his paw into your hand.

Over time, continue with *hit* practice to indicate *hit* wherever your hand may be. Begin by standing in front of your sitting dog, extending your open hand and commanding *hit*. Then have your dog *hit* while he is in a standing position. Move your hand out to the side, away from your body and command *hit*. The goal is to have contact made, wherever your hand placement may be. Make your dog stretch and work a little to get to *hit*.

Next, we will work to transfer the *hit* command from making contact with you, to making contact with whatever and wherever you choose. Because we are changing the context of the exercise to an object rather than touching you, be sure to position yourself low and directly in front of your dog. Hold an object, such as a book, in your hand and command *hit*. Continue over time, as you did before, to make the dog work and stretch to reach the object as you train toward more difficulty in body positions. Eventually, work toward placing the object on the floor, on a table or bookcase, indicating with your index finger and commanding *go*, *hit*, with success.

For a softer, more precise targeting, we train the dog to make contact with the nose rather than the paw. This alternate contact we call *touch*. We begin with our hand flat and fingers together and gently make contact with the palm of our hand to the dog's nose as we name *touch*. Immediately following contact we treat the animal. So, the excerise is; palm of flat hand to dog's nose . . . naming word *touch* . . . immediate treat. Repeat this several times.

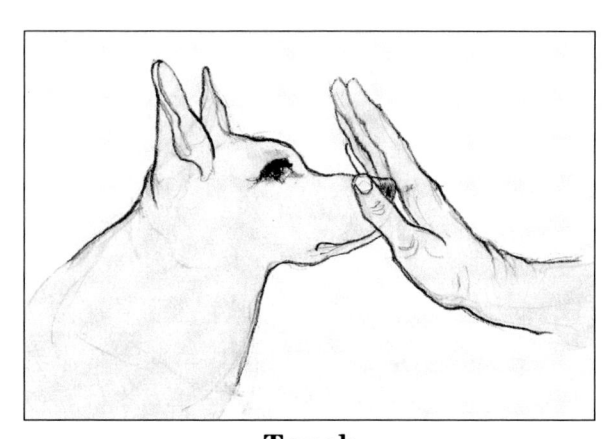

Touch

Next, hold your palm just in front of the dog's nose and with a slight, encouraging pressure from behind his head, guide forward so that the nose makes contact with your hand. Name *touch* and treat as before. After reptition of this gentle pushing, the dog should be able to reach forward and make contact with nose to palm by command alone. Remember to hold your palm quite close to the dog's nose until it is clear that the command word ***touch*** has been recognized through practice and naming. Once that is accomplished, begin moving your palm farther away, alternating high and low placements until the dog's nose hits your "target" reliably.

We then transfer the touch of the dog's nose from your hand to any object you may indicate, in the same manner as the **hit** exercises we just learned with the dog's paw. All the practice you have done in **doodling** excercises, by indicating body positioning with your index finger, will help the dog have a clear understanding of where to go and what to **touch** or **hit**. A dog, well practiced, will be able to approach any object on the command **"hit"** and strike it with his paw and on command **"touch"** make contact with his nose.

OUT IN THE WORLD

In reality, all of the time and hard work that goes into training an animal for service work can really be boiled down to two things. First, the things or tasks the animal can perform for the benefit of a person with disabilities, and second, his *behavior*, reliable to a fault, under any circumstances, while he is doing those tasks. Of those two aspects of training, the most important by far, is how the animal behaves. We can partner a service animal who may not be tall enough to hit a light switch or strong enough to do brace work. We can never place a dog in service who cannot heel when walking at your side or remain still and quiet in public places. *Training to be out in the world is not about what the dog does, but rather, who he is.*

Out in theworld

This section of training is specifically for those who are training service animals out of a specific need of their own. In the State of Ohio where our training takes place, we are lucky to be protected by statutes that understand a service dog in training has certain rights of access to public places, just as a certified service animal would. I would suggest you investigate your own state laws as they may also enhance the protections outlined by the Americans with Disabilities Act of 1990. A better suggestion is to go to places you know and talk to restaurant owners, store owners, your bank and your dentist's office. Tell these people you are training your service dog, that you would never compromise their establishment by bringing your dog there until he was ready, and that you are prepared to leave if he causes a disruption. Remind everyone that once the dog is certified he'll be with you all the time anyway, and finally, that it's just like training an intern to be a doctor; these dogs can't learn what it's like to be out in public if you don't get them out in public places. I have trained service animals for years and can count on one hand the number of times we have not gained access to the kind of training environments we need.

We begin with your readiness to enter the world with a dog. That will be based on how confident you are of your dog's behavior through all the training work that you have already done. Do not jeopardize your relationships with establishments in your community, until your dog is ready.

As a minimum, he must heel on a loosely held leash at your side. He must respond to "sit, down, stay, come, leave it" as commands, the first time and every time you require. He must not vocalize. Out in the world, this is a working animal. Service coats are available online and you should use one. Before entering the world, even on walks, **go to work** and the dressing of a service coat is the best rule for behavior. The dog should not be allowed to socialize. He is only allowed out in the world because he is attending to you.

The first outings I always suggest are to the bank and the library. The most important things these places have in common are quiet people and a low level of distractions. My favorite beginning exercise is to go to the library and head for the area with computers. I sign in, move to a computer station, put the dog in an **under**, **down**, **stay** at the desk and take a little time to check my emails.

When I'm finished, I tell my dog to **stand**, **heel** and we head out the door. It's a great first trip. Banks offer the same quiet surroundings with a higher level of attention demanded from your animal. He must stay at your side and sit patiently as you fill out deposit or withdrawal slips at one counter, and then move with you through the line to the cashiers, stopping and sitting next to you each time the line slows down. The third place I like to go early on is the waiting room at my veterinarian's office, and that is just for the very opposite reason. It is a place of high distraction in a very controlled and understanding environment. I just go and sit in the waiting room with my dog in a **down**, **stay** and let the ins and outs of the office happen as I focus my dog to **look** and reward him for his good behavior. I suggest starting this by checking first with your vet's office for slower, less hectic appointment times. Eventually, anytime you go out should be well tolerated by your animal. The bonus of training in the veterinarian's office is developing a dog that is never afraid to go there. Any trip to see the vet will be just another visit.

A local community college, particularly any classroom dealing with special education or physical or speech therapy issues will certainly be a sympathetic training ground for you to take your dog if you approach the professor personally. We have had great success in being welcomed into classrooms so our dogs could sit quietly under desks and audit a class or two!

Once you have permission, begin by arriving early to settle yourself in the back of the room and avoiding, at least in the beginning, the hubbub of hallway traffic and scurrying for seats. Always move slowly toward adding more hustle and bustle to the experience.

Go for a 2PM lunch at a quiet restaurant to start, not the local fast food joint at high noon. Sit at a corner table and position your dog, out of respect for the establishment, under your table and out of the way of busy waiters' feet. Add the distractions of peak dining hour slowly.

I'm often asked how to know where you should be practicing with a service dog in training. Where should I take my dog? The only true answer is to look at your own life. Our goal is always to train your service dog to serve the needs specific to you. So, the answer is, take him everywhere.

Finally, a few tips for dealing with the untrained public when you are with your dog. Most people are familiar with the rules of etiquette in dealing with guiding eye dogs. The same is not necessarily true for those with the seen and unseen disabilities that other kinds of service dogs assist. Be protective of your animal and the necessity to maintain his attention at the exclusion of others. Have a thick skin and learn this phrase, *"No, I'm sorry, you can't pet the dog. He's working now."*

DISTRACTIONS

The true test of any animal's training is how he behaves under duress. How reliably can we translate what a dog knows or seems to know is required of him, when we throw a distraction into the mix? Will he break from a **down**, **stay** command if a toy ball rolls under his nose or a juicy steak is brought into the room? Will he chase a cat or a child on a bike? While it is imperative that a service animal be rather immune to the stimulation of distractions, any animal's behavior can be improved by this same training.

Distractions

You have already been taught and have practiced the tools you will need. The cornerstones for dealing with any distractions are your command words **leave it**, **stay** and **look**. These are the controls your dog already knows. Make sure all of the command words from our basic training stay practiced with increasing levels of distraction.

Understand that to your animal, a distraction is generally either an unknown anything, a very interesting something or a fast-moving everything.

The unknown anything

My list of "unknown anythings" starts with hats, gloves, scarves, facial hair, eyeglasses, and umbrellas opening and closing. "Noisy anythings" are usually vacuum cleaners, tools, airplanes, fireworks and other big bangs.

If you had raised your pup holding him on one hip, wearing glasses, a moustache and a baseball cap while you vacuumed the floor in your home under the flight path to O'Hare International Airport, those distractions would just be another day at the ranch. While specific noise distractions tend not to be an issue for the well tested puppies we choose to work with, the point is that dogs need to have things known. If the world you are sharing with your dog is narrow and restrictive then more of life is unknown to him. It's your job to let him meet his first umbrella and his first hammer and nail.

Ultimately, it's your job to choose a puppy wisely, using the techniques we outlined. Noise sensitivity is particularly important to test for in puppy hunting. But you can't possibly test everything. If a new or strange anything comes up, we turn the unknown into the known, slowly and with confidence that the dog will adapt with positive reinforcement. Take the unkown hat and hold it in your hand. Let the dog sniff and explore. Put the hat in your lap, on your shoulder, on your foot and head. It's just a piece of material like the shirt and pants your dog sees you wear every day.

A very interesting something

There are lots of things your dog would like to have that we simply can't allow. The last inch of our cat's tail is high on the list of what our dog Moose would like. These distractions are a matter of training with adherence to our control command words as the situation calls for.

1. **Food**, other than what you actually give your dog at mealtimes, can be a distraction. If what he is eyeing is

"people" food, then the decision is easy. He can't have it. You must always have your dog in a *down*, *stay* when there is any person eating; that is at regular mealtimes when he is calmly under your table, and in the TV room when the family is eating popcorn and watching a movie. When food comes out, the dog goes down. An accidental piece of popcorn falling on the floor allows an opportunity to command *leave it* as you pick up the morsel. If the food is his, you must enforce the practice at all times of *sit*, *wait* as you prepare his food and *look* as a command before you release him to *go eat* and point to his food dish. Treats are rewards for a specific behavior that you have asked him to perform. Treats are never given because he's passing by, because he looks cute, or because he gave his paw to you when you hadn't asked for it. Train properly and food will not be a distraction.

    2. **Other animals** can sometimes distract your dog. I always suggest the free training ground called your veterinarian's office. Go sit there, controlling your dog in a *down*, *stay* and keep his attention as needed with *look*. Reward your dog's good behavior. Don't forget to practice *leave it* as an exercise for anything your dog is not allowed to have, ever. That includes practice in a *sit*, *stay* in the

park as the squirrels run by.

Some animals your dog comes in contact with may present a different situation. If your sister's family is staying for the weekend and have arrived with their dog Sparky to keep your dog company, you may want to allow some monitored play. That means that your well-trained service dog is allowed to play in the yard (never roughly in the house) with his weekend visitor. The only condition is this: when you say **come** the play stops and your dog responds to you. Be sure, as you practice this that the reward for coming to you when called is huge. Give enormous praise and a great treat. Proving his allegiance to you over another animal is very high level commitment. Show your appreciation and be sure to release him back to play with his weekend friend. You don't want him to think that your call means his fun is over. Just call him to you with a great treat and lots of praise at intervals during his playtime. If he won't come to you when called, then this kind of play can't be allowed until he has been trained while on a leash to respond to you even in the face of this kind of distraction. Use the leash to reel him in if his response to **come** is not immediate. You can't give a treat for this corrective exercise, but you should praise him and release him to play again, while still holding the leash. When he will break his play to come to you, give lots of praise, a treat and move to a longer leash. Use this same exercise until he understands that to continue playing he must come when called.

3. **People** are sometimes the most interesting something. They smell so great and their pockets may be filled with treats. We want our dogs to like people. In some ways it is a sign of how well our dog has been treated by the people they have already met in their lives. They feel excited and interested in this new person who may be their next best friend. It is important for a service dog to *never* seek attention from others when in his service coat and every dog needs to learn an appropriate way to greet

a stranger. The first rule is one that you should have instilled in your dog from the beginning. There will be no love or attention, no touching or affection shown, unless your dog is sitting or lying down. Your dog should always be at command in a *sit*, *stay* when anyone approaches. Practice with friends at all times that no one touches your dog unless he is sitting, and when he is in his coat that he not be touched at all.

If you choose to have someone else touch your dog while his coat is on then be sure it is attached to a release command from you. We don't want a service dog to break attention. He must wait for your command to leave your side. We use the name, *go say hi* and point to the person the dog is allowed to see. Again, even when released, the dog must sit in front of the person who has been given your permission to engage him.

Fast moving things

It is a long-standing practice that if your pet dog Beulah gets out of your control and is running loose, in order to get her attention you should move rapidly across her path of vision and then start to jog away from her. The theory is that Beulah will follow you, because dogs naturally chase things. This Beulah trick has worked for me about 50% of the time. I'm taking a guess that about that same percentage of dogs are excited to the point of distraction by fast-moving things. Think of people walking briskly and children riding bicycles. These are things that happen outside. These are the distractions you come across when you are walking your dog.

A service dog should be in his service coat and at work attention when out on the street. As leader of this partnership, it is your responsibility to look ahead and survey the landscape. Know where you want to go and be prepared to command *sit*, *stay* as you see a group of kids on roller blades coming fast around the corner. Have your dog *stay* and *look* at you until the commotion has passed and then reward him for his good behavior and attention.

Fast moving things

There is only one great equalizer when taking any dog out in the world on a walk. Service dog or well trained pet, it all comes down to *practice, practice, practice.* The better you want your animal to behave and the more comfortable he will be in any situation is exactly equal to the time you spend practicing what you expect him to do.

Apparatus practice

Puppies that grow up in families using wheel chairs and walkers, IV stands and gait trainers, are as accustomed to these items as televisions and telephones. If apparatus is added into the needs of the family be sure to introduce your dog to them as you would any unknown thing. Before a dog can heel with a child in a walker, he must first learn to heel. Before he can do retrieval to a wheelchair, he must learn to retrieve. Training for skills with physical apparatus is an accommodation to the basic skill. Teach the skill first, then as the dog grows accustomed to the apparatus, the transition will be made easily.

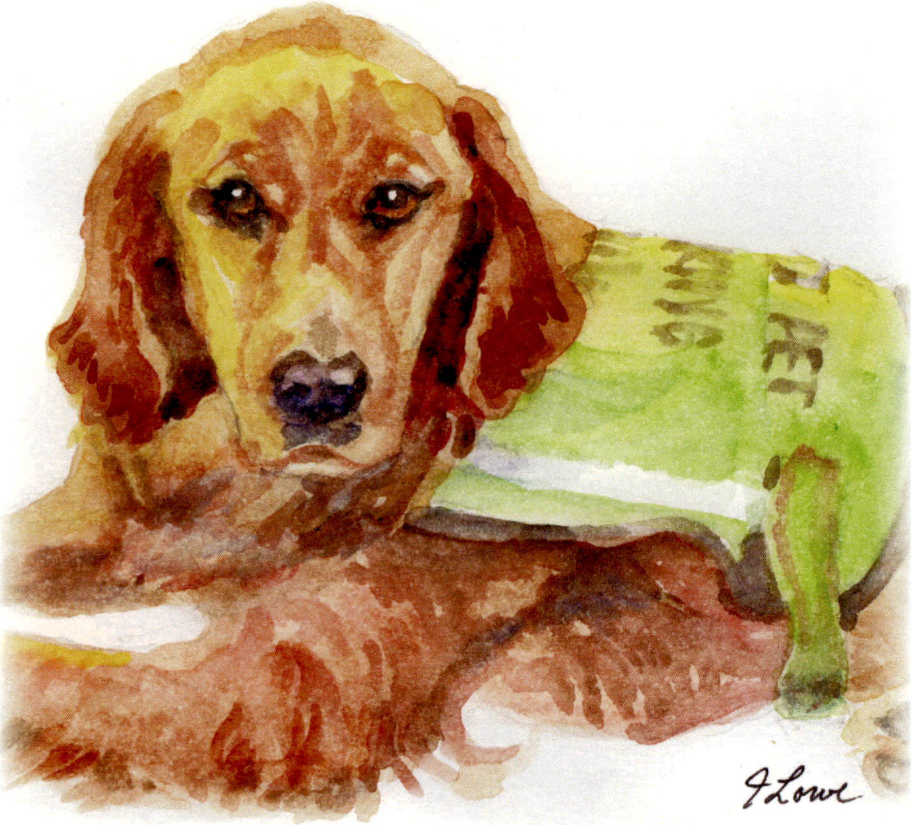
J Lowe

WEANING FROM TREATS

We have taught you to rely on the training reinforcement of offering praise and a treat to mark the moment of your dog's successful behavior performance. If you want the dog to do something again, just give him a treat and he'll do the same thing to get another. It's a great system, very positive and it works. The question is, do you have to live the rest of your life with doggie treats in your pockets? The answer is no, and we'll talk now about how to get the dog food crumbles out of your clothes.

Weaning your dog from food treats is really a matter of how consistent you have been in giving your dog treats as all his skills were being formed. The pattern is as follows: we have named all of the dog's naturally occurring behaviors, those we want him to keep doing and we have lured him into doing, and some other behaviors that we could name, too. We name and name and name until recognition occurs. The dog finally gets the notion that the noise "sit" or hand signal with bent arm that is made means, *that thing I do when my bottom hits the floor—the big bonus is, I get a treat!*

After recognition, we have the training period that develops these activities into habits. That is when the animal gets to trust, like the sun rising in the morning sky, that if he sits at the command he recognizes, he will get your praise and a treat, and life doesn't get much better than that. He understands what you want, he does it, you love him *and he gets a treat!* It is this habit-forming phase, done with consistency he can count on, that develops behavior.

Remember when you were a child? Your mother told you every night to brush your teeth before you went to bed and then one day, and for the rest of your life, you just did it. That transition—to doing something without even thinking about why—is the development of behavior.

So, if you have been generous and diligent in giving

treats and reinforcing those habits that we want to make second nature, we can start weaning from treats. We train dogs to sit at a door before it is opened by giving a treat for this. One day we will walk to that door and as our hand reaches out to touch the knob, the dog will sit and we haven't said a word. Or the dog will go to the door first and sit and wait for us to get there and open it. The dog now behaves that certain way. When I go to my desk to work, our dog will come and lay at my feet without me asking. He now behaves that way.

Weaning is simply a matter of variable reinforcement. You must up the vocal praise factor as you vary when you give a treat to every second or third or tenth time a behavior has been practiced. Remember to occasionally slip in two treats in a row. We don't want the dog to think there are never any treats in his future. The key to weaning away from treats is not to be stingy with treats while you are turning habits into behavior. And even now, with one of our service dogs working a long day of classroom visits or errands to run, I bring a few treats. Nobody wants to work for free forever.

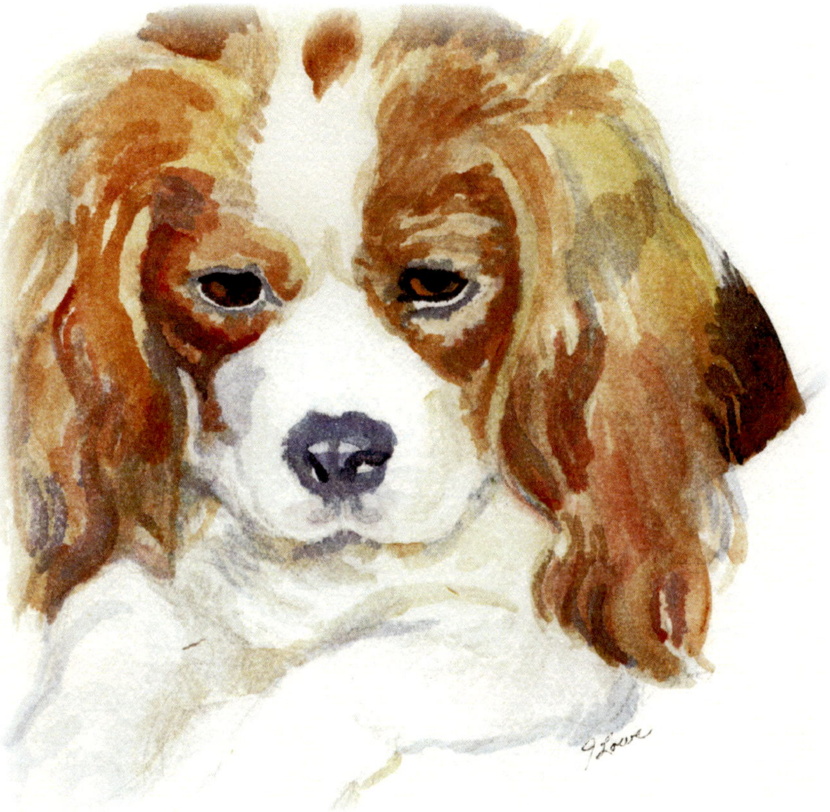

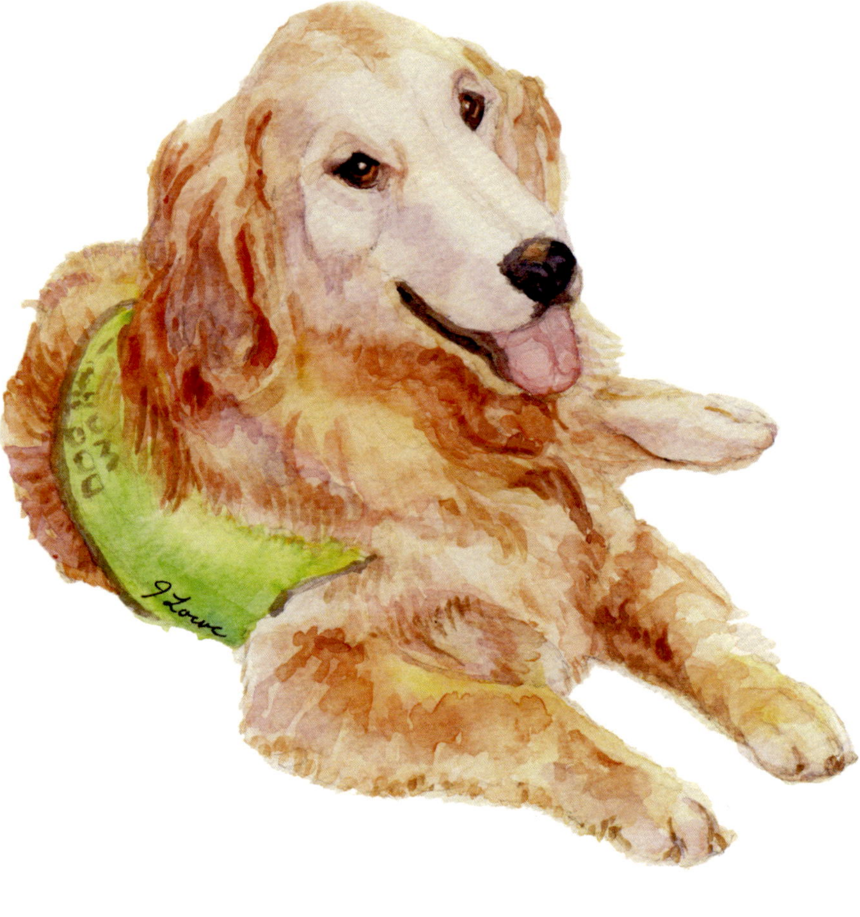

ADVANCED TRAINING

This section outlines more specifics of mobility service animal task assignments. We are interested here in connecting the dots between the commands already acquired and the skills the animal must achieve.

COMPOUND DIRECTIONS

Skill performance is achieved by teaching your dog to understand two or more of the things he already knows how to do in a predictable, repeatable series. He learned his first compound direction early on when we were training in housebreaking. ***Let's go potty*** meant going to a specific door in your home and sitting there to wait to be let outside where he was expected to go out to a specific place and urinate. That's compound. In the same way, we will fulfill the task assignments a mobility animal must excel in by forming repeatable patterns and streamlining the number of words and /or hand signs we use to communicate what we want.

TUG COMMAND SKILLS

The tug strap you have been using in intermediate skills practice will now be attached to the handle of the refrigerator and to any doors and drawers you may need assistance from your animal in opening. Do not go on to this advanced level of performance until he has demonstrated the ability to tug firmly and release quickly from the strap. Tug commands are for rigid-handled doors. Lever-handled doors will be addressed in the next section. Doors with knobs that turn are not categorized as "accessible" and must be replaced with a lever to be included as a task assignment.

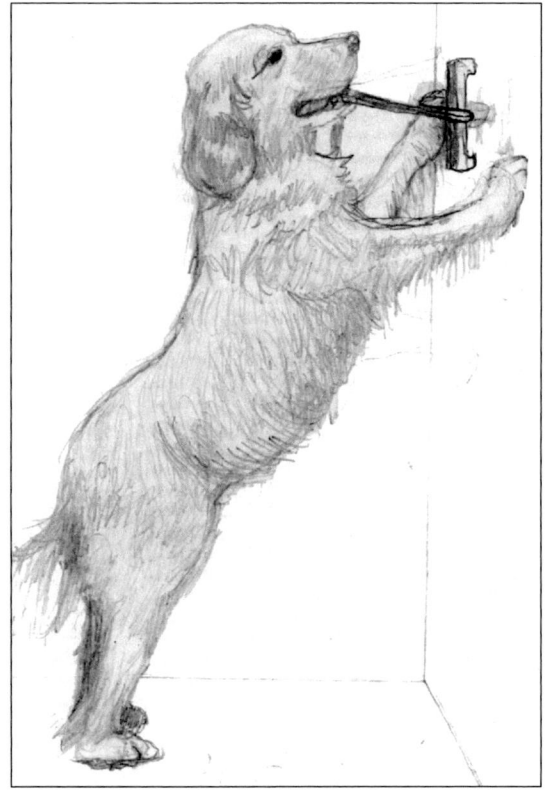

Tug

The first practice should be using a cabinet door that

has an easy release. Find a door that is easy for the dog to reach and will take a minimal amount of actual tugging force for the dog to be successful in his task. The same strap that has been used for tug practice and that your dog is familiar with is brought through the door handle. The loose strap end is brought through the loop end you had been holding in practice. Pulling on the loose end will now tighten the loop firmly around the handle you want your dog to tug.

 Begin by holding the accessible end toward your dog as you command ***tug***. As he pulls successfully the door should pop open as you name ***door*** in an enthusiastic voice and treat your dog. Next, practice pointing at the strap instead of holding it directly toward your dog. Point at it and command ***tug*** with the same enthusiastic ***door*** and treat at the successful completion of the task. Once your dog is able to grab the end of the strap with no assistance from you and will reliably tug and open the door, streamline the exercise by pointing to the strap and using the single word ***door*** to command this task. Our next exercise is the refrigerator door. We move to this door next because it presents an opportunity for the dog to learn to use a different, more intense amount of physical force to achieve success. The first exercises with an easy to open door taught him exactly what you wanted him to do. Now we will give him an opportunity to figure out how hard he must work to get the job done.

 Attach the tug strap in the same manner to the refrigerator door handle. You may begin this new door exercise by holding the loose end of the strap toward your dog. In many cases, that will not be necessary. Your dog will have a clear picture of why the strap is there. He will probably be a little surprised that the door doesn't spring open as before, with a gentle tug. Say the command, ***tug*** and as the dog exerts some force on the strap, help him out a little by using your finger to help break the air lock of the door as you give your second word command, ***door***.

Be very enthusiastic at his success and give a treat. Each time you practice this exercise wait slightly longer to offer your help. Have him work and tug a little harder before you intervene. Always be sure his efforts end successfully. Always use the command word **door** as the door opens up. He will learn to tug hard enough to accomplish this task entirely by himself. As soon as the entire process can be done alone, streamline the command sequence to pointing at the strap and using the single command, **door**.

Make sure during this process that you mix in exercises with the very easy door he learned first. We want to reinforce what the command **door** means over and over again, while he is figuring out how difficult it may be sometimes to get it done. Once the very easy door teaches what to do and the very difficult refrigerator door puts the force necessary into context, any door handle with a strap will be accessible for your dog with practice.

HIT AND TOUCH COMMAND SKILLS

All hit and touch tasks require the dog to perform a hitting motion with pressure from his paw or nose. The most common task assignments are closing the refrigerator

Hit

door, light switches, doorbells, wheelchair door access pads and lever door handles. Once this striking motion with force is learned, you may apply this skill wherever it is needed.

Practice, up until now, has taught your dog to put his paw or nose where you direct. We began with placment into your hand and then transferred that skill to his ability to place his paw or nose on any object you might hold in your hand.

Finally, that same object was placed apart from you and the dog was directed to touch or hit that same object on the floor, placed on a table or wherever it might be. Now we need to specifically pattern the things we will need the dog to make contact with for us in the future.

A lever door handle is usually our first hit skill because it is within easy reach for your dog. Put the dog in a sit in front of the door and then indicate the end of the handle with the command, *hit*. As the end of the handle is hit the door will release and you may name this *handle*, with great praise and a treat. We choose a new word for the

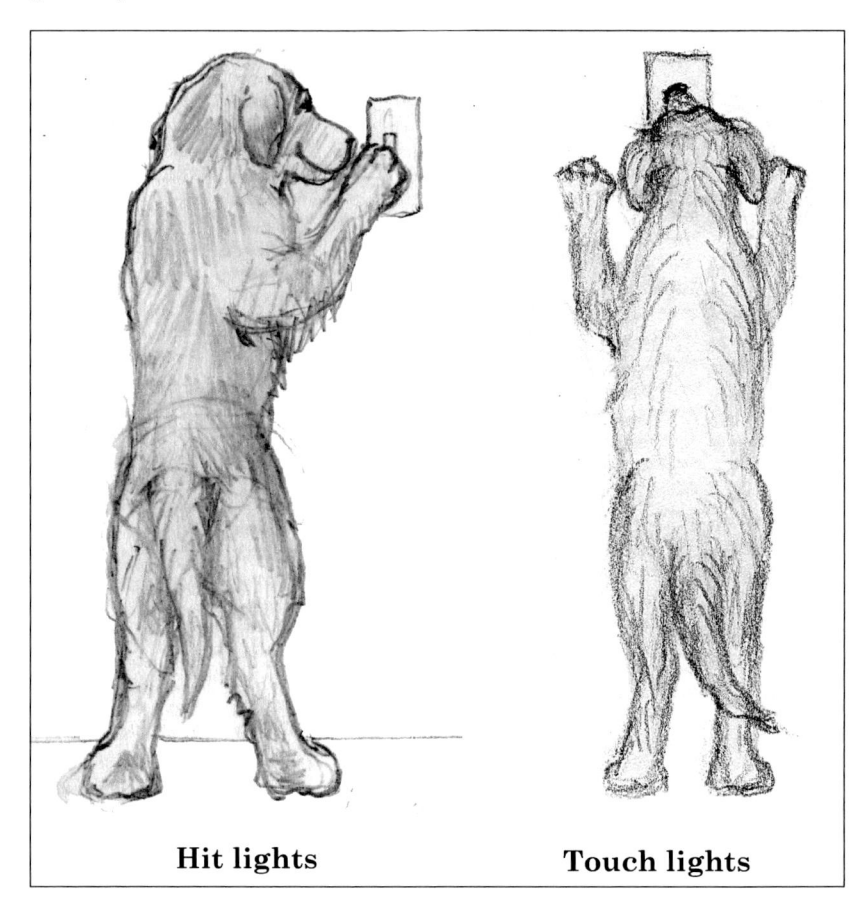

Hit lights **Touch lights**

opening of a lever door handle because *door* is the word we chose to use for *tugging* open something. Once the dog will reliably *hit* the lever to open the *handle*, you may streamline the command to the single word *handle* while pointing where you need him to go.

This progression of skills is transferred to each of the subsequent touch tasks. Point first to the doorbell and command *hit*. Continue to indicate by your insistent pointing that the dog should continue to strike the object with his paw until the bell is rung.

At the point of success, enthusiastically name **bell** or whatever target you are working on and give your dog a treat. During practice you may want to protect the wall area around light switches or use the softer **touch** command, directing your dog to use his nose and mouth. We use a large plastic food container lid with an area cutout of the middle to encircle the light switch as the "target". Continue to work toward reliability in completion of the task and the precision to hit or touch the right spot with the first try. When you are able, move toward using the single command words, **close, light, bell, pad** as the situation calls for.

RETRIEVAL

I hope you have been working all along on the very basic building blocks we began early in our instructions. Your dog must already know the command words, *take, hold, bring, give* and *drop* for service caliber retrieval work. Solid retrieval skills take time to develop. Consider the fact that most of the mobility service animals we place are two years old before they are in the home of their partner. That means two years of training has taken place and consistent practice in retrieval commands has been a part of that training.

Retrieval

Name recognition

Exercises in name recognition refer to the dog's ability to retrieve and deliver an object to a specific person. This begins by having a consistent and specific name for everyone in the household and may include naming those additional people with whom the animal has regular contact. If there are children in the household, then the adults will name themselves **Mom and Dad** or **Mommy and Daddy.** Use whatever name your children are already calling you. In that way, whenever the word **Mom** is used, it will always mean the same thing.

You may begin name recognition practice by attaching your name to all *come, bring* and *give* commands: *come to Mommy, give it to Daddy.* Identify yourself in connection with all the command practice that brings your dog toward you. If you are able to practice with another person, sit across from each other at some distance in the same room. Practice sending the dog with an object, back and forth between the two of you while using your identifying names.

Place a set of keys on the floor. Instruct the dog to **keys, take it**, then point at the position of the other person and command **go, give it to Lisa.** Your training partner should then reinforce this command with the instruction **bring it to Lisa** and show the hand signal for **give** to the dog as he approaches. Once the dog has delivered the keys, be sure to offer a treat and praise. Soon the dog will enjoy this game of bringing an object back and forth between two specific people so that he can claim his treat from each one.

We add more complexity to the exercise by putting more distance between the two parties involved in training. Pick a larger room to work in or an "L" shaped space where the dog has to turn a corner to find his delivery destination. Eventually move to two separate rooms or spaces connected by a staircase.

When you work in practicing name recognition, only use those people who have ongoing and consistent interaction with the animal. It is unreasonable to expect your dog to remember who Uncle Harry is, if the gentleman only comes for dinner at Easter and Christmas.

Placement

If you have been counting the days until your dog is able to pick up the dirty clothes from the floor and place them in the hamper, then placement practice is what will help you accomplish this feat. Placement is the retrieval skill of taking an object *somewhere* rather than to *someone*. This is accomplished in exactly the same way that we identified you by a name. To your dog, you are the thing called **Mommy**. Now we will show him the thing called **hamper**.

Be sure to start this series of commands with a hamper that is lower than the chin level of your dog when he is standing on all four feet. We do not add the complexity of jumping up or reaching into anything until he has firmly grasped the desired end result of placing something into the hamper. We begin by sitting on the floor, your dog standing in front of you and the hamper basket in between the two of you.

With a practice pile of clothing items to your side, command your dog **take it** while pointing to an item. Place the hamper under his chin and command **drop it, dirty** while you tap the inside of the hamper with your fingers. Once the item is released into the hamper name **dirty** and be sure to offer a treat and praise your dog. Never use the hamper as anything other than a receptacle for clothing items. It is not a toy. The hamper has one single purpose, which is the delivery spot for your dirty clothes. That message will be easily communicated to your dog.

As the dog becomes reliable in releasing the clothing item into the hamper you may begin to move away from positioning the hamper directly under his chin. Move first, sitting next to the hamper and then practice the same exercise while standing up. Increase the complexity by gradually moving away from the hamper and by separating the pile of practice clothing a bit away from the hamper as well. Eventually you will be able to direct your dog to pick up a single item and take it to the hamper from some distance.

During my first experience with this activity I was very diligent in naming each item of clothing as I trained the dog to place them into a hamper. I remember announcing, **sock, take it** and **shirt, take it**. I tortured myself with finding simple words to identify each item; undies, T's, it became ridiculous. Now I use the one word command **dirty** to indicate clothing on the floor, because if it's on the floor, I'm fairly certain it's dirty.

With practice, streamlining your choice of command words makes the end result you desire much easier for the dog to understand. We begin with*, take it* and*, drop it, dirty*. Those commands must always be used to mean the same behavior to your dog. The pattern should develop that ***dirty*** means to pick it up and to put it in the hamper. ***Dirty*** is always and consistently one complete activity to your animal just in the same way we will teach all the steps to bring you a bottle of water from the refrigerator, with our ***tug*** command. Eventually, the single command ***dirty*** will suffice to initiate and complete the entire task.

Placement skills can be attached to any number of retrieval based activities. Use the same method of introducing the final destination for an object. Car keys may be placed on a shelf near the door or toys put into an open toy box. The training sequence is the same once you have determined the end result you desire.

Object identification

With consistent naming and practice, your dog will be able to correctly identify and retrieve an object by name. We specifically train the dog to bring on command, his own leash, coat and the telephone. This skill is no different than your dog's ability to find his own treasured ball or rubber bone from some unknown place in your house with the offhanded mention of "Get the ball." In fact, the retrieval of the leash, coat and telephone is somewhat easier, because these items should be kept in an accessible and designated spot.

Begin by naming the leash as we did in our very first basic skills exercise. Hold the leash in your hand and offer it toward the dog's mouth with the command ***take it, leash***. Always praise and treat success. Next, place the leash on the ground and repeat the process ***take it, leash***. Our next step is to place a dissimilar object on the ground about two feet away from the leash. Choose a neutral object such as a spoon or pen. Do not use a toy. With both

Object identification

objects on the ground point at and command *take it, leash*. Treat and praise your dog. Continue to practice by switching the positions of the two objects. Put the leash on the other side of the spoon, move the items somewhat closer together. Continue to indicate, by pointing, which item is the leash as you command *take it, leash*. The next step is to stop pointing and rely on the amount of practice and name recognition to have developed. Simply command *take it, leash.*

With success, you may practice adding an additional item to be named. With a new item, always go back to the easy first step of offering the item from your hand as you name it *take it, phone*, then ask for retrieval from the ground with no other item there, and finally from the ground with a neutral item next to whatever you are naming. Eventually, place both named items on the ground with the neutral item in between them as you continue to practice. Having both named items will provide complexity to this exercise. For the first few times, help your dog by pointing to the item you are naming. As you choose to add additional named items, always go back to at least a few easy repetitions from your hand and as a single item for retrieval from the ground. Be sure to place a neutral item between each of the named items you will ask your dog to retrieve.

For items you *frequently* need, such as your telephone or the dog's coat and leash, we can ask for retrieval from a specific place. Once your dog recognizes these, or any item by name simply show him where they are kept. Have a hook or counter top where his leash and coat are always kept and a specific tabletop where the telephone is kept when not in use. From close proximity point and ask your dog, **phone** and hold out your hand with the **give** hand sign. Treat and praise your dog. With success you can move farther away from the table as you command, **phone**.

You may use your placement skills training to have your dog return these named items to a specific place when not in use. Just as we named the hamper, **dirty,** as the place for dirty clothes, decide on a name for the spot you will keep your dog's leash and coat. If it is a basket near the front door, name it **basket**. Work through the same steps of placement exercises as you did before and soon you may ask your dog to put these items away in their **basket** when you arrive home from a day's outing or return your phone to the table.

EMERGENCY PROCEDURES

We can put to use all the wonderful service skills of retrieval, tug, hit and touch commands to enable training specifically designed for an animal to set in motion emergency procedures and perhaps lifesaving attention. Choose and prepare for the procedures that will be pertinent to your own needs. This training is for a real emergency and should be practiced for an exact and speedy response from your dog. Remember to reinforce successful completion of these tasks with great praise and treats. We suggest three basic areas for you to consider *find, get, call*.

Find

I generally suggest this emergency procedure when dealing with the needs of children. A child in pain or distress is very likely to have one interest, finding Mommy. Anyone can use this exercise to initiate the dog to seek out a named person. We will use the dog's understanding of name recognition to achieve our goal. You may choose the appropriate named person based on the need in your household.

We have practiced name recognition of all of the important people in your dog's life. Exercises included retrieval skills for specifically named people, beginning with the person very near and advancing to contacting that person in a different room of the house. This practice was done with the person commanding *bring it*, of an object they wanted the dog to deliver to them.

Name recognition of a specific emergency contact person should be mastered in this same way. We work through the retrieval skills process to initiate going to a thing named *Mommy*. It is important for the emergency contact person to accept responsibility for naming themselves in all interactions with the animal. In addition, we now begin the exercise of one trainer moving through the house excitedly and with great enthusiasm with the dog, and as we walk we name our movement *find Mommy*. When we arrive wherever Mommy may be in the house, we enthusiastically name *find Mommy, find Mommy*, and Mommy should give great praise and treats. Continue with practice as you move excitedly with the dog toward Mommy and gradually command the dog *find Mommy* once recognition has occurred. Begin when the dog is standing within sight of the target, *Mommy*, and slowly add complexity as you send the dog to *find Mommy* from any distance. Mommy should always show great enthusiasm for being found.

Practice should be pertinent to the existing conditions of the person with disabilities in your household. A child with disabilities may not be alone without supervision at any time during the day. The alone time may be exclusively during the night. Practice with the dog should then be geared toward moving to *find Mommy* from the child's bedroom to the parent's bedroom or to the room in your home where the family gathers to watch television after the children are in bed. The emergency contact person, whether Mommy or someone else, must always respond to the dog's enthusiastic approach. If you have not called the dog to you, but rather he comes bounding toward you from somewhere in the house, you must always respond by going to check on the condition of the person to whom the dog is providing service. Finally, a dog, even one with exceptional training, is not a substitute for an intercom, room monitor or periodic human surveillance during the unsupervised hours of a person with disabilities.

Get

The skills of tug and retrieval can be combined in a variety of compound directions to produce an animal able to locate and access emergency medical supplies. In the final section "How Compound Can Directions Be", we address the specifics of combining multiple steps to achieve this goal. If retrieving emergency medical supplies is a service feature important to your household, there are

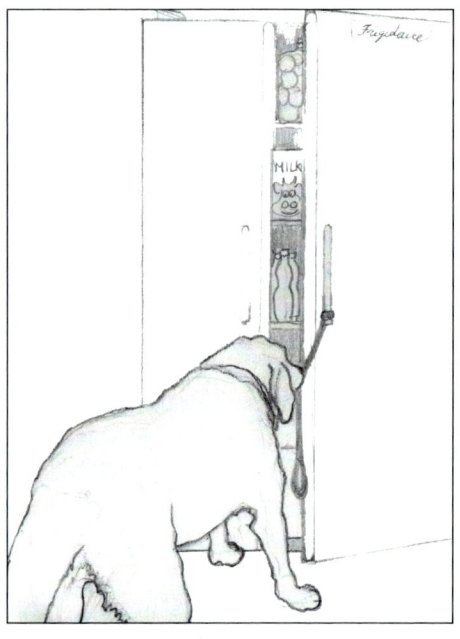

Get it

some things to keep in mind.

Specific, consistent behaviors are the easiest to teach and the most reliable for the dog to perform. Keep your emergency medical supplies in one place. Have them packaged in a container easy for your dog to get to, easy for your dog to grasp, and in a box or bag sturdy enough to withstand some wetness from his mouth or the accidental pressure of his teeth.

Dogs do not administer medications. It is your responsibility to receive the emergency container your animal has brought to you. You must take out the medication and you must take the right dose. Our suggestion is always to have a single emergency dose packaged for your animal to bring to you. In that way, you never have to worry about spilling or dropping additional medicine that your dog may accidentally get into. You would use the necessary medication and when feeling better, you could repackage and return it to its proper place, ready for any future occurrence.

Call

If the only access for emergency assistance is outside the home, the skills of retrieval, hit and touch may be used to your advantage. We always suggest training to include object identification and retrieval of a portable telephone. We strongly encourage adding the training to place the

Emergencies

telephone back to a standard location each time you have used it. If an emergency strikes, you simply can't afford the wasted time in hunting for the telephone. Practice with your dog for a speedy response to the ***phone*** command. For added security, you may want to equip your home with a telephone that features an automatic dial button. These can be pre programmed with an emergency number of your choice. Hitting the button will automatically dial and connect you with a medical emergency service or even the police or fire department. Use the sequence of touch skills to have your dog practice the place on the telephone and the amount of force needed to activate the automatic dialing feature. Name the hitting of this button ***help***, or some other word of your choice and practice, practice, practice. Make sure this practice includes sending your dog to this particular telephone from any location. ***Help*** will mean that specific button on that specific phone.

PUBLIC TRANSPORTATION

Public transportation is a big hurdle. We have to first solidly acquire all of the skills for your dog to be with you in every public situation. You have taken the dog to lunch at a quiet little spot at 2PM. Public transportation is Burger King at noon on wheels! The challenge is to find or make the opportunity for the commotion and

Public transportation

distractions of this exercise possible for your animal. We have to find a way to make this unknown situation a known commodity. We have some suggestions.

    Start with asking a friend for a ride. You and your service animal will ride in the back seat and your friend will drive. This is simulating taking a taxi cab ride. Try and pick a friend for this favor who has had little or no contact with your dog. For practicing riding on a bus, we have had great luck working with our local schools. Once the school day begins, the buses are parked for many hours a day in the school's bus garage. You can obtain the location and phone number from your local school administration office. We have actually gotten excellent results just dropping in. I'm certain the appeal of the beautifully well behaved dog at our side has helped. Explain that you are training your service dog and that bus practice is what you need. I have never been turned down, not once. The dog will have a chance to walk on and off the steep bus steps, he will hear the air lock door opening and closing and he will sit under a bus seat with you. I have, once or twice, been lucky enough to have off duty drivers volunteer to role play being strangers on the bus and taking us for a spin around the parking lot.

    Airplanes are the last testing ground. If you have been practicing out in the world in college classrooms and hallways, as we suggested earlier, this experience should translate easily. Once your animal can walk by your side unaffected by the commotion of change of class time, the bustle of an airport should seem quite familiar. What we really have been training and practicing for is that connection between you and your service partner that tells him, wherever he is and whatever is going on around him, as long as he is with you and paying attention to you, he is just fine.

    The last step of actually practicing getting on and off an aircraft has been made easier by many airlines. Check with your local carriers to find out when they are holding their next "practice night" for service dogs. It is a service now offered once or twice a year. Find out when it is available and take advantage of the practice opportunity, even if you have no trip planned yet. The time you take gives you and your animal a chance to test drive your skills. It also gives you practice in the specific procedures of your local carrier.

HOW COMPOUND CAN DIRECTIONS BE

Training compound directions is purely a matter of patterning a task. That means, finding a repeatable series of actions that fulfill an ultimate goal. Just as we first taught our dog to touch our hand with his paw, then an object in our hand, then that same object set apart from us, then any object we pointed to, and finally a doorbell. Now we have an animal with the command word **bell**,

Compound directions

that knows to hit the button near the door.

We trained our dog to open the refrigerator door using all the steps of the ***tug*** command. We could add on to that task by asking the dog to bring a bottle of water to us in the following pattern: With a bottle of water easily accessible inside the refrigerator, the dog is commanded ***door***, a skill he already knows. Standing near, we then point to and name ***water***, command ***take it***, and command, ***give***. We treat and praise our dog. This pattern must be repeated until success is reliable.

Next, we work toward eliminating many of the individual command word steps. Say your command word ***door***. After the refrigerator is opened, simply point toward the bottle and command, ***water*** holding out your hand to receive it. Treat and praise your dog's success. Repeat this process.

The next transition is to stand near the refrigerator, point and command, ***water***. Your dog will open the refrigerator and retrieve the water as you asked. Complexity may be added as you slowly practice by stepping further and further away from the refrigerator as you send your dog for ***water***. Eventually, just as he learned how to find his bathroom door from anywhere in the house, you will be able to send your dog for water from your cozy seat in front of the TV.

In the same way, your dog can easily be taught to bring a designated emergency medicines container from the refrigerator or a drawer, or to bring you your slippers, if you like. If your emergency medical supplies are, in fact, stored in the refrigerator, we recommend training to retrieve this item first. If water is necessary to take your medication, then keep a small bottle of water inside the emergency kit. Make retrieval of everything you need a one-step command.

Any number of steps are possible to attach toward the completion of a single task, as long as we work slowly with the same exact sequence of behaviors. Start each compound exercise by figuring out each small step and naming it. Names become commands and success will follow. New compound directions are best begun with a task your dog has well mastered and with a close physical proximity to you, so we are adding complexity a little at a time. As we streamline the number of steps and words we use to command behavior, keep your eye on the final result in mind. If the goal of the task is to bring you water or open a cabinet for your emergency box of medications, have in mind the ultimate single command word for the entire process. All the steps necessary will eventually be the command ***water*** or ***box***. That single word will be the trigger for whatever steps are necessary to complete the task.

Dogs Don't Speak English

SO SORRY, BUT I DON'T SPEAK ENGLISH!

A FINAL THOUGHT

If you are lucky, training your dog is a life long process. Lucky in the potential for continual skill improvement and in building an impenetrable bond with your animal. He will learn as long as you keep teaching. He will follow as long as you maintain your position as leader. This is accomplished through behavior reinforcement by reward and by consequence. You don't have to be a "dog whisperer," or know a secret language. There is no mystery or magic involved. We have told you how to pick a puppy with a wonderful temperament and disposition, a high potential to follow your lead, and the attention necessary to learn. We have offered a training method of consistency and kindness that has worked over and over again as we prepare dogs for mobility service to the children with disabilities who are waiting. Most importantly, we have left nothing out. There is no secret ingredient missing. We want you to feel empowered and able to do this yourself and have a dog to meet whatever level of need exists in your family. Just remember, talk less, do more. **Dogs don't speak English!**

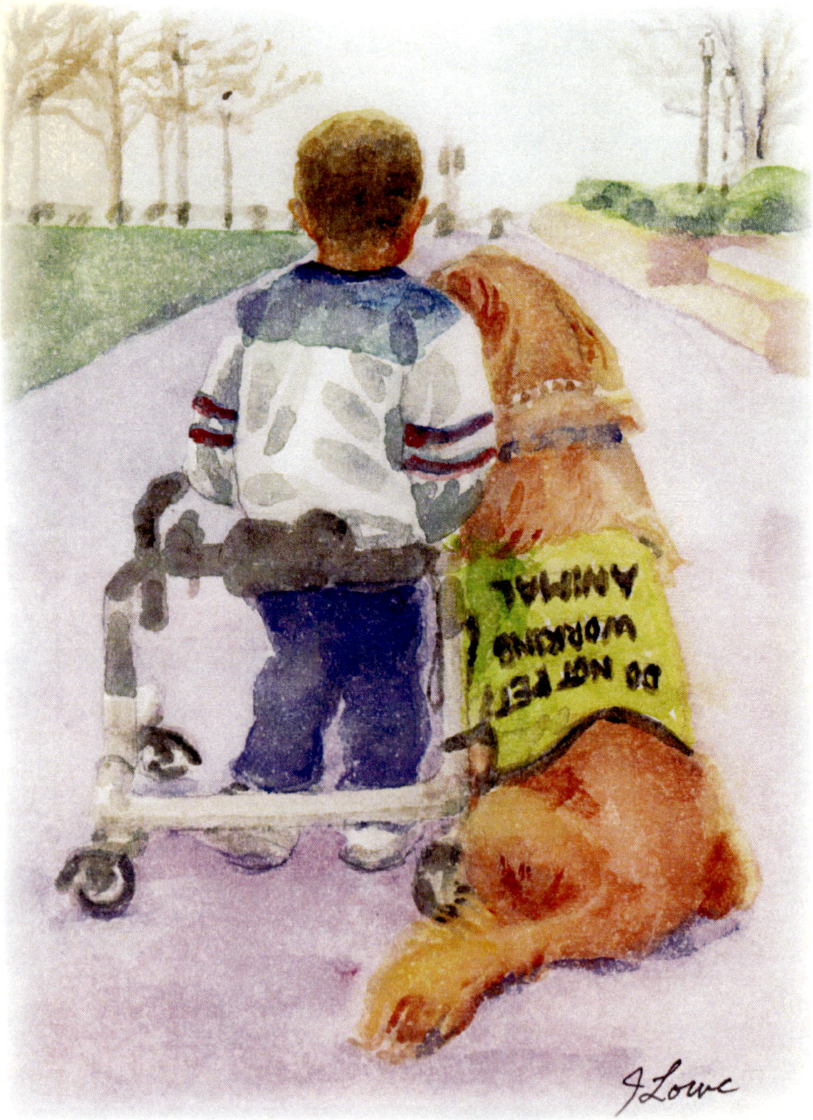
DO NOT PET
WORKING
ANIMAL
J Lowe

For more information about Working Animals Giving Service for Kids, please visit our web site www.wags4kids.org, or contact us by mail at 112 East Center Street, Berea, OH 44017.

Our mission of providing better access to, and increased availability of, mobility service and skilled companion animals to children with disabilities, is supported through the generous contributions of individuals like you. Please consider making a tax deductible donation.

Photo courtesy of Ellen Harris/Cleveland Jewish News

About the Author
Wendy Nelson Crann is the founder and Executive Director of W.A.G.S. 4 Kids. A second generation dog breeder and trainer, it is her belief that the same method of training developed to prepare animals for mobility service work can be used by anyone. Her experiences include training of both pure and mixed breed dogs, wolf hybrids and behavior modification for problem behaviors and rescue dog socialization issues from trauma and mistreatment. Her hope is to empower families to choose a dog wisely and train it to meet whatever need exists.

About the Artist
After a career as an award winning artist, art teacher and medical illustrator, JoAnn Lowe is delighted to be working on the W.A.G.S. 4 Kids project. Her paintings hang in private collections, corporate offices and hospitals. In addition to her great talent as an artist, JoAnn has raised and trained three certified therapy dogs of her own. This project has combined her love of dogs, kids and art.